UNSAFE

FAITH

Wilson Family,

I miss you all!.

Love,

In a moving and miraculous story, Mike Paulison traces a journey to bless the "least of these" that will move your heart and stir your faith. In the context of intense spiritual warfare and the obstacles of a shattered nation, God's Garden arises to bring blessing to Haitian children and to the surrounding community. The events that planted this place of grace can only be attributed to the work of a risen Savior and to His body, the Church, compelled into action by His lavish love. This story will awaken your desire to make active and ongoing missions an integral part of your story.

—Michael W. Newman
Author, *Hope When Your Heart Breaks* and *Gospel DNA: Five Markers of a Flourishing Church*, www.mnewman.org

Great book! Well-written. Tremendous accounting of God's presence and work. Inspirational and heart-warming. Brings great awareness to challenges all over the globe.

—George Dyer
Two-time Super Bowl-winning Defensive Line Coach for the Denver Broncos

Buckle Up! *Unsafe Faith* is quite a ride. Mike's story and the story of Mission Experience is so compelling because it actually happened, and because, from the first chapter, you get the distinct feeling this could become your story, too!

—Greg Finke
Author, *Joining Jesus on His Mission*

Mike Paulison has written a book that is riveting, engaging, suspenseful, and heartwarming. It will capture you right from the beginning. You will be struck by the abject poverty that exists in Haiti, as well as the lawlessness which impoverished conditions often create. Pastor Mike put himself, reluctantly, in harm's way with the very real possibility of physical injury only to be protected by God's grace.

It is a story about abandoned kids—children who have little hope only to be rescued by the sheer tenacity of Pastor Mike and God's will. It is a true story and one that reflects child abandonment, human suffering, sacrifice, and triumph. It will capture your imagination and fill you with spiritual conviction and lasting hope.

—Tom Putnam
Chairman and Founder, Fenimore Asset Management, Inc.

God's call is always life-changing, if we only listen and be open to the move of God's Spirit. Pastor Mike shares a gripping tale of how a short-term mission trip he didn't want to make into a country he never wanted to go to transformed his life and ministry into a mission he could have never expected and could not resist. This story is an amazing journey of trust in God's leading with many unexpected twists and turns. It's the story of lives changed by the love of Jesus, not only in Haiti, but by those who responded to a very needy mission field. It's a wonderful testimony to the power of God still at work in the world today!

—Rev. Dr. Gregory S. Walton
President, Florida-Georgia District, LCMS

UNSAFE

FOLLOWING GOD INTO THE UNEXPECTED

FAITH

MICHAEL PAULISON

TENTH
POWER

TENTHPOWERPUBLISHING

www.tenthpowerpublishing.com

Design by Inkwell Creative

Softcover ISBN 978-1-938840-44-9
e-book ISBN 978-1-938840-45-6

10 9 8 7 6 5 4 3 2 1

This book is dedicated to my wife, Ellie, and my daughters: Abigail, Maddie, and McKenzie, and the entire Mission Experience staff and missionaries.

This is not just My story. This is Our story.

The love of Christ compels us!

TABLE OF CONTENTS

FOREWORD

It is not the critic that counts; not the man who points out how the strong man stumbles, or where the doer of deeds could have done them better. The credit belongs to the man who is actually in the arena, whose face is marred by dust and sweat and blood; who strives valiantly; who errs, who comes short again and again, who spends himself on a worthy cause; who at the best knows in the end the triumph of high achievement, and who at the worst, if he fails, at least fails while daring greatly...

THEODORE ROOSEVELT

MINISTRY IS NOT FOR THE FAINT OF HEART. Ministry is messy because people are messy. Ministry in the best of circumstances will break your heart and sometimes even your spirit. Pastor Mike has chosen an even more difficult path— or more accurately, God chose this path for Pastor Mike. He leads a ministry in one of the darkest, impoverished, and despairing countries in the modern world. He has witnessed men do unimaginable things and seen God perform miracles in response.

Despite operating in one of the messiest settings possible, Pastor Mike and Mission Experience persist. They persist because messy people are worth it. Messy people are Jesus' kind of people—they know they are broken; they know they need a Savior.

Pastor Mike is in the arena. He has had his heart broken. He has been let down and betrayed by people he's trusted with his very life. He has seen the highest of highs and the lowest of lows. His hands are marred by dust and sweat, and his soul is battered and bloodied. He is truly following in the footsteps of his Master, Jesus. Jesus got his hands dirty and his heartbroken too. He warned us that if we took up our cross and followed Him, as Pastor Mike has done, we would suffer the same fate, "If the world hates you, remember that it hated me first. The world would love you as one of its own if you belonged to it, but you are no longer part of the world. I chose you to come out of the world, so it hates you. Do you remember what I told you? 'A slave is not greater than the master.' Since they persecuted me, naturally they will persecute you. And if they had listened to me, they would listen to you." (John 15:18–20, NLT). Pastor Mike presses on because he loves people in general and the Haitian people specifically.

God has laid a Haitian shaped burden on his heart that

he cannot escape. He never asked for this burden (in fact, as you will read, he expressly asked God not to place the burden or responsibility of Haiti on his heart—God did it anyway). Nevertheless, Haiti is a part of his heart and soul now. The children and people of Haiti are his worthy cause, and as you read this story, it's likely they will become your worthy cause too.

Now that I have extolled the virtues of Pastor Mike and the ministry he leads, make no mistake—he is a human being like you and me. He doesn't have superpowers. He questions his decisions at times and has the same doubts and fears as every other pastor and ministry leader. He is simply a man of faith and obedience who believes the things God tells Him, loves as Jesus loves, and follows the calling God has placed on His heart. He dares greatly and is spending himself on a worthy cause—building God's Kingdom among the people of Haiti.

As Pastor Mike shares his story, it also becomes clear that he's not a "Lone Ranger" in ministry. Of course, God is his primary partner, but he also has a team of people (family, friends, and ministry partners) working with him to change the world for Christ.

When I first met Pastor Mike and was introduced to Mission Experience and the orphanage in Haiti, our church was in the process of prayerfully considering who God wanted us to partner with to make the greatest impact for His Kingdom around the world. It was important to us that we partner with an organization that embraced a few key principles. We felt God calling us to be part of a ministry that looked beyond short-term mission trips—that was engaged with locals who would be able to sustain the gospel work after a team of foreigners had returned to the comforts of home. We wanted to build personal, lasting relationships with the people we were ministering with. In that same vein, we wanted to be a part of a global ministry that empowered people to change their culture themselves.

Our church and my family are personally involved with and support Pastor Mike, Mission Experience, and the orphanage in Haiti because they champion these ministry principles. As you will read in these pages, they don't run an orphanage—they empower and resource local Haitians to operate an orphanage and school. Ministry teams come not to rescue but to help the local ministry and to expand their own Biblical worldview. They aren't rescuing Haitian children by adopting them out of Haiti—they are rescuing Haitian children by educating them in Haiti, giving them practical life skills, sharing the love of Jesus with them, being an involved part of the community, and praying that this next generation of Haitians will change their country with the love and grace that Jesus has shown them. I believe this is the right model for global ministry—equipping, empowering, and engaging people in their culture, sharing Jesus with them, and watching God do the rest.

Every member of my family has been to Haiti—some

more than once. It's hard work—physically, emotionally, and spiritually. But it's a worthwhile endeavor, a worthy cause, and a high calling that will change you and your worldview forever. You will fall in love with the children, the Haitian people, the culture, and the joy of the Lord they express in even the hardest times. It will change you forever.

I would follow Pastor Mike into the darkest places on the planet because I know he has been there before. As I read the story of Pastor Mike's adventures in Haiti, I cried and I cheered. My faith has grown for my own God-given adventure. I am proud to stand beside Pastor Mike in the arena—together, side by side with the full armor of God, proclaiming the gospel of Jesus to all who need it. It's messy.

It's worth it. After you read this story, I invite you to come join us in the arena...

—Pastor David Baumgartner
Senior Pastor, Pinecrest Community Church
Parker, Colorado

What you will encounter in the pages of this book is a story as old as time. Throughout history, God Himself has led His people through both deep, dark valleys and onto high summits where one cannot help but bask in the light. God continues to lead His people each day. This journey includes times of great trepidation and grief—when faith is strengthened by the very presence of God holding His people tightly in the darkness. It also includes some of the most joyous times one can experience—when there is only celebration over what God has accomplished. Mission Experience, and those who have worked as a part of this organization, have experienced both the valleys and the mountaintops. As God continues to lead, may we follow well.

My journey with Mission Experience Haiti began even before I knew it existed. As the mission pastor of a large congregation, I have many encounters with people and organizations who are potential partners. Our congregation has been blessed to have many long-lasting mission partnerships in our home area of Southeast Wisconsin and in several countries around the world. While our mission partners are widely varied, both in the places they serve and the work they do, each relationship began in a remarkably similar way. A "random" introduction.

In the Spring of 2015, I came into my office to find a message written on my desk that said, "Mike Paulison," with his phone number listed. My senior pastor had known Mike since their Seminary days, and after they had a conversation, Keith asked me to connect with Mike. "You two speak the same language," he said. I still remember that first conversation with Mike. We spoke for over three hours as if we were lifelong friends. Mike began to tell the story of Mission Experience (ME) in Haiti, and the situation they were facing as the ministry was going through a new beginning. I remember thinking to myself, "I guess I'm going to Haiti."

A few weeks after this initial conversation, in June of 2015, I was on a plane to Port au Prince with a small team to explore ME with Mike. There were eight of us. Since we were an exploration team, we didn't do a lot of things a normal mission team might do. We had some small projects, but our days were mostly spent seeing the ministry, meeting the leaders, and praying together about what our role might be moving forward. The Lord captured all of us that week. I left knowing that there was simply no way I could not participate in the work God is doing through Mission Experience Haiti.

Since that initial trip, God has led me, our congregation, and ME, on an amazing journey together. We have been through some dark valleys—losing the properties, not knowing how to continue. We have been led to some high mountaintops—I remember standing in the open field which now houses God's Garden, and watching God provide ME with a new property and the funds to purchase it. Over our next several mission trips back to Haiti, our congregation has witnessed God work through Vacation Bible Schools, Teachers Conferences, and building projects. Through these experiences, God has worked to shape a community in Haiti. He has also taken more than 35 individuals from our congregation and shaped them into missionaries—in Haiti, and at home. Still even now, He is shaping each of us who now call the children of God's Garden "our kids." Many return to Haiti as often as possible. Others are now leading as members of the ME board of directors. Still others have found ways to use their professional skills in new ways to serve the children at God's Garden. The Lord's work through Mission Experience is far from finished. Wherever the Lord leads, may we follow Him well.

—Rev. Dr. Christian Wood
Hales Corners Lutheran Church
Hales Corners, Wisconsin

*Send us your volunteers, and we will
send you back missionaries.*

—MIKE PAULISON

CHAPTER ONE

"God doesn't call us to be comfortable.
He calls us to trust Him."

—FRANCIS CHAN

"Life begins at the end of your comfort zone."

—NEALE DONALD WALSCH

IT WAS ONE HUNDRED AND FIVE DEGREES outside with one hundred and ten percent humidity. I was sitting in the back seat of a fifteen-passenger van filled with twenty-five people. The body heat alone would have been unbearable. The van engine was already overworked, so the air conditioning was almost non-existent. Sweat drenched my shirt and poured uncontrollably down my forehead. The small, battery-operated fan in my hand was virtually useless, but it at least moved the air right in front of my face. I was exhausted from extraordinarily little rest the night before. The meager sleeping bag that I was using for a bed did not provide much comfort on the hard tile floor. Plus, having to sleep under the no-see-um mosquito netting allowed for minimal air flow. "How did I get here?" I had told God I was willing to go anywhere in the world to serve Him, except for this one place. But that one place is where I ended up.

In 1997, the church that I was serving in Sterling, Colorado was feeling prompted by the Holy Spirit to move beyond local and national missions to provide volunteers to serve on a short-term international mission trip. Today, short term missions is a two-billion-dollar a year business, but in 1997, the modern movement was just beginning. There were groups like Youth with a Mission, which had led young adults on six-month mission tours internationally for years, but short-term mission trips had yet to gain much traction as a mission strategy. A team of five were prompted to meet and pray about where we thought the Holy Spirit might be leading us to serve. After a season of research, there seemed to be three options open to us. The first was with an organization that worked with orphans in Russia. The second was a ministry that led teams to Haiti, and the third was enlisting people to serve on a boat that would float down the Amazon River, stopping at a variety of locations to minister. I remember having a long conversation with God about this trip. I told God I would go serve Him anywhere on the globe that He called me, but I did not want to go to Haiti. For years, I had watched the commercials that we have all seen, showing poverty-stricken children in Africa and Haiti with bloated bellies covered with flies. These images ripped at my heart and I knew that I was not the right person to go to these destitute locations. Certainly, God had others that were more prepared and equipped to serve than me in these places. I believed that God had called us all to missions, but surely God would not send us somewhere that would wreck our hearts or threaten our safety. I had responded to the call on my life to be a pastor and I was just starting to enjoy some success in the congregation and community I was serving. I was now willing to serve overseas, but I had my limits. I rationalized that God would honor this simple request.

The team we had assembled to serve consisted of four women and myself. Upon learning that the trip to the Amazon involved potential encounters with large snakes and venomous reptiles, the women were less than enthusiastic about this option. Then, upon further research, we realized that the Russian destination was no longer an option. Haiti was the only door that remained open, and everyone was enthusiastic about the trip, except for me. I was now preparing to visit the one place I had told God I did not want to go; however, I yielded to the Spirit's prompting. I thought to myself that I could handle one mission trip to this impoverished nation and then return to the comfort of my ministry, with perhaps the only cost being a monthly check to support the work with orphans in Haiti from a distance.

In July of the following year, we left the comfort of our homes in Colorado to join Forever His International (FHI) and the director, Stan, for a two-week mission trip to Haiti. Little did I know that it would change my life forever.

We arrived on a hot July night at the airport in Port-au-Prince. Outside the heat covered us like a hot wet blanket. As I looked around the fences surrounding the parking lot, I saw that they were lined with Haitians staring at those who were entering their country. The noise was deafening as Haitian airport workers yelled at us and grabbed at our luggage hoping to gain a tip for their help. It was all so overwhelming.

We had been warned not to release our luggage and to closely follow the group as we moved toward the parking lot, so we gripped our bags tightly as the Haitian porters yelled and grabbed at them. When we got to the van, we loaded the bags on top and pulled a rope through all the handles so no one could grab one and pull off the luggage. Pastor Janvier, the Haitian pastor we came to serve alongside, decided to ride on top, just to make sure no one would have a chance to steal any of our bags. We climbed in the van and drove out onto the packed streets of Port-au-Prince. As we left the lights of the airport, the darkness grew thick with the absence of electricity. The smell was a combination of coal fires and the mass of humanity. It seemed like every person living in the city was out on the streets.

I would learn later that Haitians live in an outdoor culture where most of their time is spent outside. The evening provided a respite from the hot afternoon sun, so the Haitians were ending the day with their friends. While the nighttime was a respite for the Haitians, to me, the heat and humidity of the night was anything but a relief.

It had been predetermined that we would spend the night at a missionary compound in the city of Port-au-Prince. The road from there to Gonaives was dangerous at night, and robberies and muggings were frequent. Our van ride was my first introduction to Daniel. He was the ministry driver. You could see the love of Jesus in his wide smile and bright eyes. He was good-natured, and we immediately became friends. After driving for about a half-hour, a man darted out from the crowd, jumped on the bumper, and leapt on top of the van. He grabbed a piece of luggage, hopped off, and started to run. It seemed that in the blink of an eye he had snatched the only bag that did not have the rope laced through the handle. Daniel stopped the van and jumped out to pursue him. As he did, I opened the side door and followed him. After only about ten feet reality set in. These were the streets of a country with which I had no familiarity. My run slowed to a trot and then to a dead stop. I looked around at the people who filled the streets as they stared back at me. Then I slowly backed up to the van and closed and locked the door, humbled by the circumstances. A few minutes later, Daniel returned with the piece of luggage in his hand. He had caught up to the man and shoved his finger in the man's back. He told the man he had a gun and commanded him to drop the luggage and walk away without turning around. The man did so, and Daniel returned to drive us the rest of the way to the compound. We drove in silence, shaken by the events. My first night in Haiti was a success! We were all still alive.

The next two weeks were among the hardest of my life. The average temperature exceeded one hundred degrees with unbearable humidity. We traveled through the country during the day, serving at local churches, schools, and orphanages. The fifteen-passenger van we traveled in was usually filled over capacity, which only made the heat worse. The only respite was when the sun went down, but the reprieve was hardly measurable in July. We slept on tile floors in a compound that only had electricity two hours a day. There were no lights or fans for the night, and we slept under no-see-um mosquito netting, which provided almost zero airflow. I was miserable. Each night, I would spray cold water on my chest, then set a portable, battery-operated fan on my waist pointing up toward my face. This would allow me to bring down my body temperature for a brief two-hour span, providing me with intervals of sleep.

The third night, I was awakened from one of my rare moments of rest by a blood-curdling scream. I ran to the window. It was clearly a woman being abused or raped. Had I heard this kind of cry in America, I would have called the police immediately and then gone myself to help, but I was in an unknown place where the same rules did not apply. I sank to my knees in prayer. My heart was breaking from an inability to help. The screaming stopped after a few moments, but it would be hours before I would fall back asleep.

During the two-week trip, my relationship grew with the mission team members, and my bond with Daniel was becoming like that of a brother. We grew closer during the many hours spent driving in the van. He seemed to care deeply about the safety and success of the team. He took his job seriously. We could not communicate clearly because of the language barrier, but we could use facial expressions. He would smirk and shrug his shoulders, and I would laugh.

It was a few days into the trip that we met Daniel's wife, Madeline, Pastor Janvier's niece. Both she and Pastor Janvier had been raised in voodooism with the expectation that they would follow the family tradition of becoming priests. Madeline had only recently become a Christian. She and Daniel had just had their first son, and she was excited about her new faith and meeting her first mission team. She spoke much better English than Daniel and would often answer questions about Haiti and her culture.

Over the next two weeks, the daily trips were over the rough, sometimes impassable Haitian roads. Twice we traveled to lead a crusade in villages. On these days, we could easily spend four hours in the van. These evening crusades were unique because the villages had no electricity. When we first arrived, the children of the community would be the first to welcome us. For some, it was their first time seeing "blancs"—people with no color. The children would run their

The streets of Port-Au-Prince, Haiti

Haitian street market

Haitian street market

hands through our fine hair and try to wipe the "white" off.

On the first crusade trip, as the sun started to go down, we set up our limited equipment consisting of a small generator illuminating one light bulb and an amplifier powering one electric guitar. The light lured out the people of the village. We sang and preached. This crusade was held under a tree where voodoo worship was conducted weekly. There was little receptivity except for one boy. Afterward, the village's Christian pastor shared how difficult it was to serve in this place entrenched in voodoo. When asked about what would happen to the young man who responded to the message that night, he replied that the boy would likely be kicked out of his house and now have to live in the church. The entire team was saddened by the hardship the boy was going to endure. We prayed for his protection and new faith.

During these trips, we often had over twenty people, Haitians and Americans, packed into a fifteen-passenger van. All those people packed into the small space made it difficult, but it provided the right atmosphere for some amazing moments. Often on the way back home in the evenings those in the van would break forth in worship. The songs would be ones that were known in both languages. In those moments I believed we were getting a small glimpse of heaven. The writer of the Book of Revelation writes, "After these things I looked, and behold, a great multitude which no man can count, from every nation and all tribes and peoples and tongues, standing before the throne and before the Lamb, clothed in white robes" (Rev. 7:9). Then John, the author, writes how they all erupted in worship. I envision them all singing before our Lord in their own languages and everyone understanding each other. It was moments like this that filled my heart with joy.

The second crusade we performed was in a distant village. We again set up the generator and the speaker, but we did not need the light in the afternoon. As the musicians played, the entire village turned out. Voodooism did not completely entrench this village like the previous one. I preached for the first time through an interpreter. The people responded positively, and it was a fantastic day with brothers and sisters in Christ from another country. Afterward, we were invited back to the home of the village pastor. As we rested there, we learned that the villagers had gathered their food and made a Haitian meal for their visiting missionaries and the entire village. When the food arrived, the members of our team looked at me and asked, "What do we do?" Stan had repeatedly told us not to eat any food that was not either made by us or prepared at the missionary compound. The problem was that Haitian water had different bacteria than we were used to in the U.S., and if the food were not cooked and cleaned correctly with bottled water, we would all get sick. I looked at Daniel and he just shrugged his shoulders and smiled. My response to the team was, "We pray and then we eat." I was not about to offend these generous people with whom we had just shared God's love.

A lesson that I was learning on this trip was how Haitians struggle with their self-value compared to Americans. One Haitian man shared with me why his nation decided to serve the gods of voodooism nationally instead of Christianity. He said, "We looked at America and saw how they prospered. We assumed that God loved the white man and hated us, so we had to choose another god." I did not want to embed this lie further in their culture, so we ate. I would become sick numerous times over my years serving in Haiti, but no one got sick on this occasion. God was merciful to us all.

Another event that really struck me occurred toward the end of the trip. On this day, the FHI director, Stan, after conversing with Pastor Janvier, felt led to go to the pastor's sister's house to share the gospel with her. She was a voodoo priestess and had never been open to the faith of her brother. The three of us decided to drive over. Upon arriving, we saw small altars with animal bones dispersed everywhere. We parked the vehicle and approached the door. The servant girl opened the door. When we inquired if the priestess was there, she said she had just left. Then she informed us that just a few minutes before, her demon had told her we were coming and that she should go. This would not be the last time that the spiritual realm would have a tangible or visible effect on our circumstances. I would never have the chance again to meet her.

When the two weeks ended, we returned to America. In the weeks to come, we would share the stories of God's love and grace with our home church. They had generously supported our trip and worked at our fundraisers. They again responded generously with ten thousand additional dollars to support the ongoing work in Haiti. I was grateful to have made it home safely. It was an experience of a lifetime. I thanked God for it, but I had no intent to return.

Solomon writes in Proverbs 16:9, "The heart of a man plans his ways, but the Lord directs his steps." As I settled back into my ministry in Northeast Colorado, Marcia, a member of our first team, approached me about returning to Haiti the next summer. I was not interested but told her I would pray. A few months later, I found myself boarding a return flight to Haiti. It seemed that God desired obedience and was not bound by my wishes. I would like to tell you that I was a joyous recipient of His call to return to Haiti. Truthfully, I was not, but there was an important connection there that I had made with the kids at the local orphanage, Pastor Janvier and his family, the full-time missionaries, and Daniel, Madeline, and their bouncing baby boy.

Upon our arrival, Daniel again met us at the airport. We embraced and exchanged hellos. God was creating an intensely personal relationship between us. The two weeks, again, were hot, humid, and long. I had not received some miraculous gift of mercy that would allow me to endure the heat easily. It seemed that I obviously was not equipped to live in a hot, humid culture.

I witnessed again God touching those we served. The

Haitian people were amazing. Although they seemed to have so little according to the world's economy, their joy was infectious. The Haitian believers I met seemed to have such deep and rich faith. I admired them when they prayed because it was so intense and personal. It was unlike anything I had ever experienced in the United States. Unlike we Americans who value order, when Haitians pray, they do so all at once out loud; it is not finished until the last person says "Amen." These prayer events could easily go on for twenty to thirty minutes. Neither prayer times nor worship services were ever rushed. On Sundays, church got done simply whenever they finished the service which could last over two hours. Once when I was preaching, I finished the message after a half hour. It was about twenty minutes worth of content with an additional ten minutes in between for the interpretation. I sat down. The pastor looked at me and then stood and preached another sermon. He could not let the people leave with so short a message. Daniel and our other Haitian friends just smiled.

Later in the trip, I would experience danger in Haiti for a second time. One day after being out all day ministering, the team returned to the compound. It had been another long, hot day and we were all ready to take a cold shower, have dinner, and rest for the evening. We arrived back, and like every other day before, Daniel drove up to the gate and honked. When no one opened it, he eventually got out and slid it open. He then returned to the van and drove it inside the compound. The team helped unload the supplies and went inside. I stayed and helped Daniel unload the remaining items. Afterward, we walked to the gate to slide it back in place and lock it. As we talked and laughed, we stepped out in the street, enjoying each other's company. Then there was a commotion down the road, and we turned to look, only to be met with the loud noise of a gun being fired. As the bullets zipped by us, I looked at Daniel wide-eyed, and he returned the look of fear. We jumped inside the gate, slammed it shut, and ran further inside. That night, Daniel did not go home for fear of his safety. We got him some blankets, and he slept in the room with the men on our team. We sat up for hours as he asked questions about America, our families, and our way of life, and we, in turn, listened to his stories about his country. It was an unexpected night of blessing.

The ministry relationship established between FHI and our church back in Colorado lasted for several years. As we grew closer to this ministry, a deep relationship was created with Pastor Janvier and with the boys at the all-male orphanage he founded. Each trip resulted in spending a lot of time with them. I was drawn to one young boy about the age of five. Whenever we came to the orphanage, he would run to greet me and hold my hand for as long as possible. On one trip, we took all the boys to a pool and purchased snacks for them. The purpose of the whole day was simply to have fun and love on them. We all played and laughed together. Most of the time, the boy was draped around me. He obviously longed for a father figure after his parents had died and I, having no children at the time, loved the joy it brought me. I silently wondered about the possibility of adoption. As I questioned further, I discovered complications because this boy had an older brother and there was no desire to split them up. I went into a season of prayer but the adoptions never happened. I was comforted, though, by the fact that I could return and see this boy in the following years. At least, that is what I believed at the time.

During the next few years, Pastor Janvier began to get involved in the Haitian political process. He announced that he was going to run for president. At first, my heart was excited because I believed in his leadership ability. He even convinced a couple from the church I served in Colorado to lead his North America fundraising efforts. This all came crashing down in the following months as it was revealed that he was stealing funds from the ministry to finance his political aspirations. When confronted, he became obstinate and reasoned that he had a right to do this because, as he said, "That is just the way it is done in Haiti." He eventually failed in his political bid, but his lack of integrity, among other reasons, prompted the full-time missionaries to leave the country. Soon, ministry ties were severed and we, along with Stan and FHI, stopped all work in Haiti. My heart broke to leave my new-found friends and the boys I had grown to love behind. I did not know it then, but I would never again see the young boy who brought my heart so much joy.

As the years passed, I maintained contact with Stan as he

followed Daniel and Madeline's lives. Occasionally I would hear how they were doing, and when they went through difficult times, I prayed for them. I did not think I would ever return. It was amazing how this country that I prayed I would never go to had made such a lasting imprint on my heart. Now it seemed like that ministry door was going to be closed. Then a large-scale earthquake hit Haiti in 2010.

CHAPTER TWO

"Sympathy is not a substitute for action."

—HUDSON TAYLOR

ON JANUARY 20, 2010, A DEVASTATING EARTHQUAKE hit Haiti, with Port-au-Prince as the epicenter. Earthquakes on the island of Hispaniola, where Haiti is located, are not uncommon, but one of this magnitude is. It hit around 4:53 PM, 15 miles southwest of the Haitian capital of Port-au-Prince. The initial shock registered a magnitude of 7.0 and was soon followed by two aftershocks of magnitudes 5.9 and 5.5. These events would have been deadly enough, but the aftershocks would continue for days, hampering rescue efforts. According to the Haitian government, over 300,000 people lost their lives as a result of the earthquake, but because of the mass graves where they buried so many of the bodies, the final count may never be known.[1]

The images that appeared on television were devastating to watch. The most famous one was the image of the collapsed palace; however, destroyed buildings were everywhere. The streets were lined with people now homeless and searching for loved ones. The country was in a daze for months. The following years would be filled with debates over the reasons for the widespread devastation. None of these arguments mattered to me however, as my heart flashed images of my friends in Haiti. I immediately got on the phone to find out if they were all safe.

I phoned Stan from FHI ministries. He shared that Daniel and Madeline were safe and now living in Port-au-Prince. He had returned to ministry in Haiti a few years ago and was partnering with them to start a new orphanage. They had several children already, but now were displaced by the earthquake. They were presently living in tents but were in the process of buying a new property. The new site would be called Jehovah Orphanage.

At this time, I was serving a new congregation in Aurora, Colorado, which was deeply invested in national and international missions. We had traveled six times to New Orleans to help rebuild after Hurricane Katrina ripped through the city. We also were sending members from our church to help serve on short-term teams in Rwanda and India. After this devastating earthquake, it was time for me to consider returning to Haiti. I had mixed feelings because of the circumstances that caused me to leave the first time.

I wanted to protect my heart from being wounded again. I was comforted with the knowledge that I would be returning to advance the orphanage led by Daniel and Madeline, and I thought my heart would be protected because I trusted them.

A mission team from our church scheduled its first trip to Haiti later that year. I was excited to return, partnering again with FHI. It would be good to see Daniel and Madeline and their son. A site now housed the Jehovah Orphanage, and the students were no longer living in tents. Our team consisted of five members, some of whom were apprehensive about serving after the earthquake. Their concerns were calmed by the knowledge that I would serve with them. Together, we would process the sights and sounds of Haiti. Many who travel to Third World countries are fearful of the danger. Life there is a day-to-day existence. The condition of Haiti before the earthquake was considered the Third World, but the quake decimated it. Before the earthquake, many people lived in homes with no indoor plumbing and slept on dirt floors; however after the earthquake, the millions displaced lined the streets and fields with makeshift shelters. As always in this country, danger could flare up at any moment. All these factors made the team members nervous.

I was sure that the Holy Spirit was leading our team to take this trip. Unlike my previous trips to Haiti, I was now eager to go on this one. I was looking forward to reconnecting with Stan of FHI and my Haitian friends along with becoming a part of this new ministry endeavor. As the trip dates quickly approached, the team studied the culture, packed, and prayed. Then I got sick. If it had been a simple cold, I would have still gone despite the doctor's warnings, but it turned into the flu and a sinus infection. I trusted our partnering ministry leaders, so I sent the team and stayed home, dejected. On my previous trips to Haiti, I went apprehensively, informing God that I did not really want to go. This time I was ready to go, and I was forced to stay home. It did not make sense to me.

Mission trip veterans led our team. They traveled safely and experienced profound moments of God's grace. Upon their return, they shared stories of the children at the Jehovah Orphanage and of the devastation they witnessed. Displaced people lined the streets. The rubble of fallen houses was everywhere. Thousands upon thousands of people had lost loved ones. The Haitians' anguish and pain were real, but in the midst of this, the team had discovered a well of joy in the children's lives and faces in the orphanage. They spent a week loving and serving them.

The night the team returned to share their stories in church, their stories moved the entire congregation. Although I had not been able to make this trip, I had decided that I would join the next trip with FHI. After the service, the father of one of my staff members approached me. He had attended church that night to watch his grandchildren perform in a children's program, which was also part of the service. John K had recently retired, and although he was not a church attender, he felt moved to ask me if he could join me on the next trip. I agreed, warning him that he would have to sit through many devotions and Bible studies, but he still felt compelled.

A few months later in 2011, we boarded a flight to Miami, where we met the other team members. This was the first time I met Stuart. He was one of the leaders for FHI and oversaw construction. He was the epitome of a good, solid, Nebraska farm boy. He was a part-time pastor who felt God had led him to be a partner in the ministry of FHI. When we arrived in Haiti this time, it had an entirely different feeling than years before. The heat was stifling, but it was not as awful as I remembered. It helped that it was not the middle of the summer. We arrived at a temporary airport, which was assembled after the earthquake. Stuart had brought tubs of tools, but there was no hassle at customs. There were still plenty of men attempting to help us with bags, but it was more organized and not a swarm of men yelling and grabbing at our luggage. People still lined the streets, perhaps even more since the earthquake, but the oppressiveness I experienced years before was gone. I wondered if something in the country had changed or if the difference was in me. When we exited the airport, we found Daniel and Madeline standing right outside, ready to welcome us. While they hugged the team members, I stood in the back. Daniel and I saw each other and smiles immediately swept across our faces. Madeline, unaware that I was coming on this trip, simply came to hug me as she had the other members. When she looked me in the

Haiti after 2010 earthquake

John on his first trip to Haiti

Mission team after playing Haitian teens in soccer

eye, recognition set in, and she started jumping up and down. "Pastor Mike!" she yelled and leapt into my arms. After the embrace, there was a new joy in her step, and she danced her way to the vehicle with the team following.

The orphanage property was in Tabarre, northwest of the airport past the U.S. Embassy. As we drove, I noticed a field situated at the hill's base leading to the orphanage. Tents made of blue tarps, provided by the United States to use as shelter, filled the field with those who had lost their homes. My mind immediately flashed back to New Orleans after being hit by Hurricane Katrina. These were the same tarps that covered so many houses in New Orleans after the storm. Many Haitian people had a hard day-to-day existence before the earthquake, but this looked unbearable. I had served previously on numerous mission teams after natural disasters in many areas around the U.S. In New Orleans, I saw ships that had been lifted by the storm and dropped right in the middle of the Ninth Ward neighborhood. I witnessed cars on top of houses and houses on top of cars in the wake of Hurricane Katrina, but I had never seen devastation like this. Crumbled buildings were everywhere. The grief and pain of the Haitian people were as thick as the humidity in the air.

This would be an emotional week for both John K and I, as it had been for the previous team. During the week, Madeline and Daniel recounted the horrors of the earthquake and the pain suffered in the following days. On the day of the earthquake, Daniel had been on the way home from the airport and stopped for gas. He went inside to purchase a beverage and then left. Minutes later, the gas station building collapsed as the ground began to shake. He had narrowly escaped danger. As horrific story after story was recounted concerning the events of those days, our hearts broke for the Haitian people.

One evening in the middle of the trip, the team sat outside in a covered area, having dinner and devotions. A light rain began to fall. We did not think much of it and continued sharing our thoughts of the day. As the intensity of the rain increased into a Haitian downpour, the team members headed to their rooms. I sat outside for a little while on the deck and watched the rain fall, taking some pictures. The next day, we awoke to another humid sunny day. We gathered to have breakfast, and Daniel shared the sad stories he had already heard about the aftermath of last night's rain. The intensity of the rain had caught us all by surprise, but those encamped at the bottom of the hill had taken the worst of it. The torrential downpour came so hard and fast that it quickly filled up the street in front of the property where we were staying. The stream turned into a river with a swift current headed down the hill. Eight people died that night in the tents occupying the field at the bottom of the hill. As the water swamped the field, they could not get out of their tents fast enough, becoming entangled and drowned. Our hearts were becoming overwhelmed with the enormity of the pain caused by the earthquake and its aftermath.

Thankfully, time with the orphanage children provided moments of joy, restoring our hearts. Fifty-two children called the orphanage home. In the mornings, while they were in class, we constructed new beds for them. Then in the afternoons we played basketball and other games and danced with them. There were a lot of children housed on a small piece of property, but they did not seem to mind. While we were there, they seemed to be full of life and joy. Our hearts bonded with all of them. John K found joy in taking the time to teach the older boys some construction skills. One day some of the boys even baked a special treat for us. It was chicken baked in bread dough. They came out and offered it to the entire team. The team members, taking seriously Stan's warning about eating food not prepared correctly, graciously declined. Stan and I decided to partake. It was delicious, but the next few days we would pay for that decision as we both got sick.

On the final night, we gathered for our last evening devotion. It was decided on this night that we would share in a time of encouragement. This was not a large team, so we took our time encouraging each person individually. Daniel and Madeline were last. They thanked everyone for their hard work and their dedication. When Madeline got to me, her eyes welled with tears. She grabbed the tissues and shared how thankful she was that after all these years, I had come back. I was part of the first team she met after becoming a Christian. Becoming a believer changed everything for her. She shared that it meant so much to her that we did not forget them. As she shared, tears rolled down my eyes. I had no idea that I was that important to her. It was an emotional time sharing the relationships God had formed.

Later that night, I went to the bedroom to talk to John K alone about how this week affected him. John K and I began to discuss the trip. He had enjoyed his experience and was excited about the possibility of returning. At the end of the conversation, I decided to address the subject of faith. We had experienced many highs and lows throughout the week, and I wondered how this was affecting his faith journey. I asked him directly about what he was going to do with Jesus. John K stopped and looked at me, and he said, "Mike, I believe. I really do believe." This moment would change John's life forever, and his decision to return on future trips would connect both of us to this small island nation.

The trips would continue to Haiti over the next few years. Our relationship with Madeline and Daniel would grow, and the love for the children would expand, as would the teams and the pieces of property. This time included a trip for Madeline and Daniel to America to share their mission in our church. We connected even more with what God was doing in Haiti. During these years, the short-term mission movement was sweeping through our nation. As it did, I felt an inward tug toward creating a program to equip short-term teams more effectively. The tug turned into a desire to start a short-term mission training school, where teams could be trained to impact the culture they entered and evaluate how the trip transformed their own lives. My desire was to help transform short-term volunteers into lifelong missionaries serving at home and abroad.

The ministry in Haiti continued to expand during this time. Another American ministry based in Nebraska sought the help of FHI to purchase a piece of property halfway between the team center site and Jehovah Orphanage. It was not large plot of land, but they planned it well. It housed a center to support future mission teams and other buildings that would support the orphan's care. Upon completing the buildings, the ministry realized that its real heart was to build but not operate an orphanage. They then gifted the property to FHI and announced the joy of their decision on their website. Then another piece of property was later added about a block away and it was named Seventy Palms. The vision for this property was to provide a housing community for the students as they aged out of the orphanage. The ministry now had four pieces of property and was growing fast. The first piece was the land that Daniel lived on and housed teams. The second was the orphanage site. The third was the site gifted to them, and the fourth was Seventy Palms.

One night, while at home between trips, I was awakened by the Holy Spirit and prompted to pray for Haiti. Images of Haiti and the children passed through my mind. I got up from my bed and went to the living room to pray for our mission endeavors. That night as I sat on the couch and prayed, I felt the Holy Spirit instill a message in my heart. I felt the prodding that I needed to share that message with the church I was pastoring so as to publicly affirm how I was being led. The following week at the end of the service, I shared what I felt God had laid upon my heart. I refreshed the congregation's memories of all the work we had done in Haiti and the children we had grown to love. We knew their stories and their names. I told them that I wasn't sure of what it all meant for the future, but now, the Spirit of God impressed upon me that I would be involved in some way in Haitian ministry for the rest of my life. At the time, I did not feel that this meant me leaving the pastorate, but I believed that there now was a heart connection between myself and Haiti that would last the rest of my life. This country that I had never wanted to serve in was now part of me.

CHAPTER THREE

*"Let my heart be broken with the things
that break the heart of God."*

—BOB PIERCE

IN JANUARY OF 2013, WE SENT IN a small mission team from
our church to continue working at the Jehovah Orphanage.
Upon their arrival, they discovered a tension that seemed to
be brewing between Daniel and Madeline and the leaders of
FHI. There was not as much camaraderie as before. Over the
next few days, it became apparent that something was wrong.

During that week, a startling revelation came to light that
gave more clarity to the evil that lurked behind the orphanage
walls. One of the team's missionaries was a counselor, and the
leader of FHI had asked her to use her skillset with the teens.
The original goal was to determine if any of the teens were
struggling from the psychological effects of the devastation
they witnessed during the 2010 earthquake. Stan, desiring

to give the teens a chance to freely talk, arranged for the counselor and him to meet with the students privately. He was fluent in Creole, so he would translate. But instead of painful memories of the earthquake, the teens shared stories revealing a hidden reality that would change the ministry.

It is typical for Haitians to be heavy-handed when it comes to children's corporal discipline, but FHI had worked hard at teaching those on staff alternative forms of correction. During the counseling sessions, the teens revealed previously inconceivable forms of physical discipline that were occurring. This harsh discipline would never happen when a mission team was present but happened frequently between trips. The teens told stories of being beaten so badly that they could not get out of bed. They shared that one young man, who we thought could not participate in team experiences on one of our previous team trips because he was sick, was really suffering from a severe beating. He had been told if he said anything to us, they would kill him. Others shared stories of how the girls were taken from the orphanage and being forced to work at Madeline and Daniel's home in a slave like manner with no compensation. On Thursday night of that week, tensions mounted as Madeline asked to speak with the team. At first, she seemed to want pity by sharing stories of the difficulty of caring for fifty-two children at the orphanage, but then in a moment, her mood changed. Her voice began to rise until she was yelling at the team to stop judging her for her actions with the kids. It was clear that something terrible had been hidden, and the darkness did not like the light revealing it. This spiritual battle intensified and left the FHI leaders a lot to address and navigate through going forward.

Meanwhile, our short-term mission's ministry efforts began to expand at home, as did my conviction that we had to become better at equipping short-term ministry teams for service. The desire to start a short-term missions training school continued to grow in my heart. The world was changing, but our method of equipping teams was not keeping up with it. In the past, missionaries went through intensive training and a linguistics study before entering the culture they would serve. This would not be possible in this case, so I knew we had to create our own training form. I examined what groups like Youth With a Mission (YWAM) were doing. YWAM would send young adults on a six-month tour. Before they sent their missionaries overseas, each student would receive a few weeks of mission training school. This was not feasible for a one or two-week trip, but why could we not create a more attainable model replicated with teams across the country? With this idea in mind, I began to work on a model, and in the fall of 2013, I would have the first chance to put it into practice.

During the spring of 2013, I began contacting individuals around Colorado with whom I had a previous ministry relationship. The goal was to find opportunities to expand our short-term ministry efforts in Haiti. I requested the opportunity to speak with a small group of like-minded people from each church. This led me to reconnect with

Doug. I had known him and his wife Leslie for several years. Years prior, he and I had served on a short-term mission team in New Orleans, and I knew he and Leslie had a passion for international missions. Doug did not seem to have any interest in going to Haiti, but since he had a heartbeat for missions, he arranged a meeting with the leaders of the church he was attending. By the end of that meeting though, the Holy Spirit prompted Doug that he and Leslie needed to go. It surprised them both, but God was preparing to change their lives. I took the opportunity to share at the other churches and watched in amazement as God inspired thirty diverse people to come on a trip together to Haiti. We committed to several training sessions over three months. It started as a time of education, but we soon realized that group building was also an important concept in preparing a team for a mission trip. The result was a group of people who had a life-changing experience that has kept many of them connected to this day.

As November approached, the team of thirty grew closer and more excited about their trip. The vast array of gifts among them revealed a unique team. There were contractors, self-employed business owners, accountants, nurses, and a doctor. They had all raised funds and collected items for the orphanage students. I was excited about leading such a talented team. As I watched the team, it was satisfying to witness the fruits of our labor in the preparation process; however, later it would become apparent that there are some events for which you cannot prepare.

Weeks before the trip, I received a phone call from Stan, the director of FHI. Since we sent teams regularly and had known each other for years, he wanted to make me aware of recent events. The unease that had started with the revelations on the previous trip had only grown. The children's abuse was even more widespread than imagined, and the beatings were more horrific than first realized. Tensions had increased between Daniel and Madeline and him, and it was evident the older children were tired of being abused. As the weeks passed, we would learn of even more deception. The education they were receiving at the orphanage was below Haitian standards, and the pledge Daniel had made about the orphanage being registered with the state was simply another lie. It is still stunning to me that even though hundreds of orphanages operate in Haiti less than a hundred are officially licensed by the State. I do not know if others have been deceived as well, or if they are simply trying to justify that their work is important enough to not participate in the long process; either way the statistic is troublesome. With tensions mounting, Madeline announced to the teens that they would have to make a choice. They could either stay with them or leave for good and go live with Stan. The problem was that Stan had never intended to start an orphanage in Haiti. Despite that, thirteen teenagers chose to leave and were invited to live at Hope Village with Stan. Our November team was preparing to work with all the children, but now we would only interact with thirteen of them.

Leslie and our girls

Steve F, James, and our kids at Seventy Palms

Stuart and Doug

After the teens departure, an exhausting legal battle ensued. The four pieces of property were divided between the two groups. A Haitian judge ruled that Daniel could stay and operate the Jehovah Orphanage and retain both the property on which it was built and the property on which he lived. The other two pieces of property, Hope Village and Seventy Palms were delegated to Stan to continue working with the thirteen teens now committed to his care. Ill feelings continued to rise as both these ministries had to exist side-by-side, operating in the same neighborhood. Stan's lawyer repeatedly assured him that the properties were listed in the name of FHI and the legal papers were being held in her office, so FHI focused on functioning as an orphanage and caring for the teens. A new problem arose as it became clear that the attorney was now also serving as Daniel's lawyer. Later, it would be discovered that she was biased toward Daniel. A Haitian man, Joseph, who had worked previously as an interpreter for FHI, was hired to live with the students and oversee their care at Hope Village. He had experience working with these teens and seemed to have a heart for children. A second man named James was hired to be the team driver. James was a man full of life, faith, and joy. He took a keen interest in building relationships with the staff and mission teams. He was the chauffeur for now but would play an important role in the years to come.

As the November trip approached, it was clear that the focus of the team had shifted. Now, they would be going to Seventy Palms to assist in building cottages that would house the teenagers and serve as a transitional community when they aged out. They also would have to help amid growing animosity. Stan and Stuart would not only have to be concerned for their own safety, but also the security of future teams.

The team arrived at the end of the first week of November, ready to work on the jobs in front of them. They all now knew of the issues that were present and the continued legal battle. There were many implied threats against the FHI staff, but none acted upon. Even so, the team kept a strict safety protocol. There was no way to determine in advance what Daniel's reaction would be to this first team in the country after the split. Stan and Stuart did a great job keeping the team focused, active, and sheltered.

My heart was in anguish at not being able to see all the children who remained at Jehovah Orphanage, and the loss of my friendship with Daniel. I remembered one little shy girl, in particular, who held my hand and followed me everywhere every time I visited. Mirlanda did not speak much, but she would always sit next to me. On one of the previous trips, I had given her a picture of myself. I would not learn of this until a few years later, but she put that picture under her pillow and prayed for me each night. She later told me that she always knew God would find a way for us to be reunited. Since FHI provided most of the orphanage funding and now that funding was cut off, we were unaware if their basic needs were being met. I feared that I would never see her and the other children again.

It was a busy week as we pushed hard to build one of the future student cottages and complete work on another previously constructed cottage. Sometimes, the teens would come to the worksite to spend time with us, but they mainly stayed at Hope Village. We did most of our interacting with them in the evenings. Through all this, the team of thirty had united. For some, their hearts were being connected to Haiti as mine was years before, but they would not know it for some time.

That Thursday was another long workday. It was hot and humid, even in November. We arrived back at the team center around 5:00 p.m., and everyone proceeded to their nightly rituals of showering and getting cleaned up before dinner. Evening meals were always a good time to process the day and allow time for our bodies to refresh after a long workday. We did not know it yet, but Stan had planned for the teens to share their stories of abuse that night. It was late by the time we got to them, but, one by one, they shared their personal journeys. Although the team was exhausted, we sat for almost two hours listening to their pain. They told horrific stories of physical abuse which included for some being whipped with the split ends of an extension cord. They shared that there were times when the beatings got so severe that the son of Daniel and Madeline, who was a friend with some of the boys, would step in and take their beatings for them. Another truth surfaced that some of the children never needed to be in an orphanage.

Their families had the means to raise them, but they had been convinced that their children would have a better life in the orphanage. To know that some had unknowingly traded life with their family for a life of abuse was yet another blow to our already broken hearts. Although there were some orphaned children there, others were being used to inflate the numbers to garner support from missionary churches. The faux walls started to fall and behind it was a picture more broken than we could have ever known.

The days ahead were hard ones as we continued to hear stories about the kids who remained at the Jehovah Orphanage. One young boy named Kerby had no family but was forced to leave in the weeks to come. Daniel could not obtain more funding and was slowly sending all the remaining kids away. Kerby finally found shelter in the home of a stranger. He would often call Stan in tears, begging to be allowed to come to live at Hope Village. The complications of the legal issues that still existed between FHI and Daniel made it difficult for Stan to give the boy permission. It would take almost a year before Kerby could return to his friends and the safety of Hope Village. The little girl and her sister I had grown close to, Mirlanda and Dieuslande, were also forced to leave but at least had a grandmother to care for them. When they had to leave, I asked one of the Haitian workers to find them and make sure they were safe. In the months to come, he found them, and we were able to make sure their basic needs were met.

A few more trips were made in the next couple of years as Seventy Palms began to take shape as a future housing community for the Haitian teens. Six cottages and a kitchen pavilion were built. Doug, Leslie, and others from the team of thirty returned to serve again. Those serving were pleased with all the work that had been completed and the advancing new vision for the ministry, but we didn't know the full extent of the evil lurking behind the scenes as animosity continued between the two sides.

CHAPTER FOUR

"If you want to walk on water, you've got to get out of the boat."

—JOHN ORTBERG

IN THE BIBLE, THE BOOK OF JAMES READS, "Come now, you who say, 'Today or tomorrow we will go to such and such a city, and spend a year there and engage in business and make a profit.' Yet you do not know what your life will be like tomorrow" (James 4:13–14a). We humans love to make plans, and I am no different. By the fall of 2013, I could feel that change was in the air. I had spoken to the leaders of the church I served and shared that my heart was changing. My passion for world missions was growing, and my desire to start a short-term missionary training school was apparent; however, the plans I was laying out were not what God seemed to have in mind.

Also in November, one of our church leaders, Keith,

asked to meet me for a drink. We had not had a chance to visit lately, and since personal time together was common, I did not expect any new revelations. We met and shared about our families and our ministry. As we started to wrap up, Keith seemed to get serious. He said that he and the other leaders had met together while I was not there. This was a surprise, but not totally out of the ordinary. He shared that they realized that God seemed to be doing a new thing in my heart. They wanted me to know that they were releasing me into whatever God was doing and that they would continue to lead the church into the future when it became time to find a replacement for me. He said that I was free to pursue another ministry as God directed. "Release me," I thought. "Release me to what?" I had no call to consider with another ministry. What was I being released to? Sure, I had the heart to do a new thing, but that could take months or years to be established, and I had to have the means to support myself in the meantime. At the time, neither of us knew how prophetic of a word this was.

By the end of the year, growing donations of tools and supplies for our next trip to Haiti flooded my garage. It became apparent that a trip to Omaha was necessary to deliver the supplies to the FHI office. These supplies could be stored there and then later sent to Haiti in a shipping container. By this time, John K had returned several times to Haiti and was willing to take the trip with me to assist. During the first week of December, we loaded the pickup and drove the long trek across Nebraska. We arrived and unloaded everything while having a nice visit and catching up on Haiti's events. As we prepared to leave, Stan asked me what my heart was for Haiti. It seemed like he was fishing with his question. He was beginning to realize that his service in Haiti may be wrapping up during the next few years, and he was trying to discern who the next leader might be. I loved Haiti and the Haitian people, but our congregation and I were involved in numerous places nationally and internationally. I had a heart for all those places and more at that moment. I did not feel like God was leading me to get so deeply involved in one particular country. I shared this. Stan understood. We shared hugs, and then John K and I headed back to Colorado.

Traveling through such a long open expanse in a state like Nebraska allows for plenty of time for conversation and evaluation. Inwardly, the discussion with Stan churned in my mind. I wondered if I missed something. A few hours into the trip, I silently prayed and confessed this feeling to God. I told Him that if I had missed something, He would need to make it apparent, and if somehow He would bring the issue around again, I would consider it. The uneasy feeling started to dissipate as I rationalized that this situation was concluded. As we traveled, my thoughts shifted to all that needed to be done at home, and the conversation with John K turned toward our next mission trip. I was making my plans but did not even consider the passage from the Book of James that none of us knows what tomorrow holds.

The holidays and New Year did not allow me time to reflect much on the conversation with Stan. Then the first week of March, I received a phone call from him. He had called to update me on all that was occurring in Haiti. The relationship between he and Daniel had continued to deteriorate. Living in the same neighborhood was challenging. Daniel and Madeline blamed Stan for the orphanage division and seemed to be determined now to make him and others feel threatened. Every movement had to be watched with a cautious eye for fear of retaliation. Stan no longer felt safe nor was he able to advance the ministry in Haiti. The crux of the phone call was that he wanted to share that he had just finished a season of prayer and discerned that God was closing the doors for him to continue to perform his ministry in Haiti. His heart broke for the thirteen teenagers who were left, but he felt like he had no choice. He would need to release them, sell the property, and then use the funds to continue to support them as best as he could from stateside. As he shared, I could feel God quicken my heart, so I proposed, "What if God would lead me to take over this ministry?" I followed with, "How long do I have to make a decision, and how much would I need to raise to keep it going for the first full year?" The list was long and complicated. I would need to start a new ministry from scratch, including enlisting people to serve on a board of directors and submitting all the paperwork for a new non-profit organization in the US. As to the funds for a transition, I would need to raise $20,000 to start a legal foundation in

Haiti and about $60,000 to cover the property's expenses, pay staff, and fund the students' education and needs in Haiti. On top of this, I had no supporting churches or ministry structure and no American staff to assist me. All of this would have to come together in ninety days. We ended the conversation with the only commitment being that I would now enter my own season of prayer.

The next week life moved slowly as I considered all that was before me. I first had to have a family meeting. After dinner one night, I shared with my family the possibility that was before us. It did not mean we had to move, but it did mean that life would change and that I would be gone more often. I asked them to pray about it. All three of my girls responded that they did not need to pray. Although none of them were old enough even to join me on a trip yet, they knew my heart. For the last seven years, they served alongside me, helping the homeless in our home city. They knew God had designed me with a heart for the less fortunate. They believed that we could not abandon these teens. First box checked.

I knew that I could not do this alone, so the next step was to discern the people who would consider partnering with me on this endeavor. The issue of having people to work beside me on a ragtag staff weighed heavily upon my shoulders. On the Seventy Palms property, five cabins had been built, but most of them needed finishing. The outdoor kitchen pavilion was up, but it needed some work to be used in the future. The security guard was presently living in a tin shack and needed a

We are not "all about work."
Missionaries playing with the kids.

Our kids

Missionary team with our kids at Seventy Palms

home built as well. Plus, in my mind, I was contemplating the need to be prepared to receive more children in the future. It became apparent that I would be unable to both perform all the leadership tasks and lead construction. The simple fact was that some of the construction was beyond my experience. I needed someone with significant construction experience.

On top of that, I desperately needed someone to help with all the organizational nightmares that were ahead. There would be plenty of paperwork to complete soon, both in Haiti and in the United States. I would also need to seek donations and keep all the records associated with an NGO (non-government organization.) All these concerns and issues swirled around in my head. This season of prayer was accompanied by many sleepless nights.

I was first led to invite Doug and Leslie to lunch. They had both accompanied me on the large team of thirty, and they had previously served on numerous short-term mission trips internationally. Leslie had experience running a mission office for multiple years and was currently unemployed. Doug was a self-employed independent contractor with numerous years of experience. When we served together in New Orleans after Hurricane Katrina, he led the construction component. We met for lunch, and I caught them up on all the events in Haiti. I shared that although I did not know if I would accept the assignment yet, there were a lot of answers I needed to have in a short period of time. I shared with Leslie that I would need her experience and gifts to make a successful ministry transition. If there was one leadership principle I understood well after years of being a leader, it was that you surround yourself with the best people who know how to do what you do not. I shared that I would have to decide soon, and I needed someone with her skill set on staff to partner with me. I asked her to pray about this, but I told her that I had a short timeframe for her to make a decision. In addition, I would need her to start right away, but I did not have any idea when I could begin to pay her. Her response and expression are as clear in my mind five years later as they were fresh on that day. She looked at me and said, "I don't have to pray. Of course, I will do it."

Then I turned to Doug. This meeting was not for Leslie alone. I expressed my concern about all the construction that needed to occur and how the plan would be to increase the number of children we helped in the future. I desperately needed assistance from someone with his skill and experience. The plan was laid out, and the request made that he also pray about partnering with me as the construction director. There were not a lot of details hashed out at this point, but at this time, it would be a volunteer position. I reiterated that I needed his answer soon and that I would like him to pray about it. His response replicated his wife's reaction. He replied, "I don't have to pray about it. I will." It became clear that God had been leading them to this point as well. Second box was checked. Now I had two people committed to serving with me, but I still had no money and no leader board. For the first time, I seriously contemplated, "What if God really wanted this to happen?"

The coming weeks were filled with me going almost every Sunday afternoon to meet with a group of mission-minded people at our partner churches. I called a leader from each congregation who had previously joined me on one of our trips and asked them to set up a meeting for me with like-minded people at their churches. Much to my surprise, each of them agreed. I had two requests for each group. The first was that I needed individuals to serve and share their wisdom on a board of directors. I was searching for leaders, entrepreneurs, and mission-minded people with a passion for impacting lives for Christ. I shared that this would not be a comfortable journey. Haiti has amazing people, and on this journey, they would have the thrill of seeing God operate firsthand; but I also shared that it was a difficult country in which to do ministry. Their hearts, like mine, could expect to be broken as well. Leadership comes at a price. Secondly, I shared the $80,000 financial goal. We were a few weeks in, and I only had about ten total weeks left to decide. The clock was ticking.

The miraculous part was that the Holy Spirit moved eleven individuals from five different churches to join me on this journey as part of the board. Many others felt compelled to be on teams that would be incredibly significant in the coming months to establish our work in Haiti. God was providing exactly what I was praying for: an extremely gifted, diverse group of leaders. I was astonished at how quickly God moved. Many of those in this group had previously started their own businesses or were leaders in their respective fields. It would be fair to say that God had already prepared them for this moment. The third box was checked. Wow!

A few weeks later, a handful of us borrowed a van and headed to Omaha to meet with Stan and the board of Directors of FHI to pray about the possibility of us starting where FHI was ending. On the way to Omaha, Matthew West's song, "Do Something", played over the airwaves. The lyrics of the song ask why God allows pain and suffering in the world, and why He doesn't do something to stop it. The song ends by stating that God has done something. He has created us to make a difference in the world. As the song ended, in silence, we all looked at each other. Could this be happening? Are we going to take this step of faith? We had leaders for staff. We had willing people praying about serving on a board of directors. The only thing in our way was a commitment of eighty thousand dollars. The total committed at this point: zero. I did not know how God was going to pull off the financial component.

The visit to Omaha went well. We experienced some powerful prayer times as Stan and the FHI Board of Directors shared what their vision had been before the present mess. They were excited that we were stepping up to start a new ministry to take over and build on the work they had begun. "Wait a minute," I thought. "We had not committed to anything yet." They shared how the May first date was a hard date and either they would put the property on the market, or we had to decide to begin. We left with no definitive answer because I still needed to find the funds. They had laid a solid foundation. The property was theirs, and there were only thirteen teenagers. This seemed manageable with God's grace.

As the weeks progressed, all the five churches started making pledges, and the individuals who had committed to serving on the board were very generous. I had only about twelve weeks to decide and three of them were already gone. I would like to be able to share with you that some wealthy donor stepped up and simply said that they would make up the difference between what we could raise and the goal. But there was no single donor. During the next two months, I spent every free moment praying and contacting everyone whose name God laid on my heart. I did not raise the funds and pledges in nine weeks. It only took six.

CHAPTER FIVE

"Be of sober spirit, be on the alert. Your adversary, the devil, prowls around like a roaring lion, seeking someone to devour."

—1 PETER 5:8

THE FIRST OF MAY ARRIVED, and the responsibilities of the orphanage were switched over to Mission Experience. It seemed to be a seamless transition. Stan had not lived in the country full time and neither would I. He had a system set up where the Haitian employees cared for the teens and ran the operations daily. The teens continued to live at Hope Village and were all enrolled in school. The first team that we brought in June went well. The employees had to get to know me better and trust the new leadership, which would take some time. The primary work task was to complete Seventy Palms. FHI had donated all their tools and supplies, so everything was in place to pick up where they left off.

Over the next few months, several teams came in and served with Mission Experience. They stayed at the team center at Hope Village and would often walk the road between the two properties. This road went directly in front of Daniel's home, but teams rarely saw much movement. I was concerned for their safety, but it was nice to have peace continuing the work that had begun. It had been a rough last year and we just wanted to advance the project.

I still worried about the almost forty children that remained at the Jehovah orphanage. My concern was that they were cared for and safe. When FHI stopped supporting them, there were no other agencies providing funds. Through neighborhood gossip, I heard they were struggling and some of the children had been sent away. I did not know if I would ever see them again.

The number of teens living at Hope Village increased slightly with the return of three of the children who had been sent away previously from the Jehovah Orphanage. Kerby had finally come back after being forced out. He returned right before the ministry transition. The year Kerby was on his own was extremely hard on him. The man with whom he lived was harsh. Now he was back with his friends and in a safe environment. It was not long until his big bright smile reappeared. The other two children who returned were the sisters. Mirlanda and Dieuslande had gone to live with their grandmother. Their parents had died several years before in a hurricane in Gonaïves, but they were blessed to at least have some living relatives, unlike Kerby. I contacted their grandmother and invited the three of them to come and visit. The sisters immediately came to hug me upon their arrival. They were shy when they arrived, but it did not take long to reconnect with the other teens. The grandmother thanked us for our concern and shared how Mirlanda had kept my picture and was praying that I would come find her one day. We invited the girls to stay and the grandmother agreed that this would be best for them. We completed the legal paperwork and our family grew.

Over the next year and a half, ministry and life advanced. Four of the cottages at Seventy Palms were complete, and because the property was larger, it was decided to move the teens and nannies there. The kitchen pavilion was finished, and a new home was built for the security guards. The ground was rock hard, and every project required the difficult task of breaking it up. It was backbreaking labor. Later, a basketball court was poured and other buildings were planned for the lower part of the property. The teams continued on a regular basis staying at Hope Village and building a welding shop there. By this time, after a season of reflection, Stuart had rejoined the ministry. He had worked hard leading the building projects at Jehovah Orphanage, and he had needed his own season of grieving and prayer to see if God would lead him to be part of Mission Experience. He was also attempting to discern what his role might be with this new ministry. We welcomed him and his experience back with open arms. He partnered both in construction and leading teams. He had the gift of encouragement and faith that we needed. It seemed like everything was advancing as planned until later that year. We did not know it then, but evil was again trying to wreak havoc behind the scenes attempting to stop the work that God had started.

Over this time, much effort and time were also required to begin the long process of paperwork necessary to operate legally in Haiti. Starting a foundation first required me getting a long-term stay permit in country and obtaining a national identity number. It seemed like every time we were close, something else was required. On one occasion when my long term stay permit was almost complete, they needed a passport size photo in a button-down shirt. I wondered where in Port-au-Prince was I going to get that accomplished. James said he would take care of it. We got in the pickup and started driving deeper into the city. After an hour or so, we arrived in a deteriorating neighborhood. We walked up to the second floor of a building, and there was a man with a camera and set. I was not wearing a button-down shirt, so I went back on the street and bought one. I went upstairs and had the picture taken. The background was white, and my shirt was light, and of course, my skin was white. Later after he developed the photographs, all the photographer had to say as he handed them to me was, "Too white, too white." On the way out, I took the shirt off and gave it back to the street vendor to sell again. This would not be the last time I would "rent" clothes off a street vendor to enter a government building. Another time I needed a pair of long pants to enter a government building because I was wearing shorts. I had not seen many Haitians my height at 6'4", so I thought this would be interesting. I went to the nearest street vendor who had three pairs of pants hanging on a fence for sale. He grabbed one pair and handed them to me. Obviously, he was at this location because I was not the only person to forget to wear long pants to get in the building. I put them on over my shorts and they fit perfectly. God provided again. Later as I exited the building, I stripped them off as a crowd of onlookers watched me. Then I once again handed the pants back to the man to resell.

During this time, the orphanage was in a transformation process. Several of the teens who were already eighteen or older began to journey out into the world on their own. At the same time, we began to receive younger children into our care. The minimum age of the children dropped significantly as many of these kids were younger.

After the foundation paperwork was complete, the next step was obtaining the orphanage licenses. Both a national license and a city license are required for orphanages to operate in Haiti. I learned that you did not need to be in a hurry because everything got done on Haitian time. In America, being on time is important, but as previously mentioned, in Haiti time is relative because relationships are the highest priority. We started with the city license and would tackle the national license later. It was again a long,

Kids praying over a mission team as they leave

Seventy Palms

detailed process concluding with a property inspection. The city officials praised the orphanage property and operation of the orphanage, so we were in good shape. When most of this was complete, I began to reach out, with the help of Stan, to the lawyer who he had used previously to transfer the name on the paperwork from FHI to Mission Experience. Stan had continued a relationship with the lawyer, and she constantly reassured him that all the legal paperwork was in her office and that she would assist in any way she could. The problem was that after numerous attempts to talk to her, she would not return my phone calls. It became apparent in the coming weeks that something was not right.

Then one day, Daniel showed up at Hope Village and asked to see me. I was not there, but our security guard relayed the message to me. Later, James and I walked over to Daniel's property. He welcomed us and it seemed like he was trying to rebuild the relationship. It did not take long, however, for the truth to be revealed. Haiti is commonly known as one of the most corrupt countries in the world. Corruption is widespread in politics, but I was about to learn how much deeper that corruption ran. I asked Daniel about the children that remained at Jehovah Orphanage. He was honest and said that it was difficult to care for them now and that only a handful remained. He had been unsuccessful in finding new funding and support. His wife was now living in the States with their new baby who needed better health care. Then the conversation turned to the properties, and

I realized why the lawyer would not return my phone calls. Daniel had manipulated her to change the names on the paperwork and put it in his name even though he had not paid for the property. Since I still had no hard copy of the property paperwork, I instantly became concerned. He had reached out to another prominent Haitian, Franz, who now had a working relationship with the American group based in Nebraska that had originally purchased and built Hope Village. He had enlisted Franz's support in his effort to steal both pieces of property. It was not long before I realized that this was a blackmail session. He said that he would not legally take action to remove us from the properties if I would once again partner with him and support him and the orphanage he ran. I refused to move the kids from the property nor enter back into a relationship with him. I left, but the war had begun.

Over the next couple of months, threats increased and Franz got more involved. He wanted to obtain Hope Village to expand his own work. He had convinced the Nebraska-based ministry leaders to support his efforts and say that they had been manipulated to give the property away. Even at this time over three years later, it was clearly stated on their website that they had freely gifted the property with no strings to FHI. Despite all the deceit, I finally agreed to a meeting in February between the three of us.

As I planned in February to return to Haiti, after much prayer, I determined that I needed to travel alone. There was no way to know what would happen in the next encounter, and I could not with a clear conscience put anyone else in harm's way. Two weeks before the trip, John K approached me. He had been praying, and he did not feel peace about my safety returning alone. He asked to go for support and requested only to remain at Hope Village. The Board of Directors was also pushing for this. At first, I disagreed, but I relented after additional conversations, and John and I decided to return to Haiti together.

Then five days before the trip I was awakened in the middle of the night with severe pain in my lower back. I knew from previous experience, that it was kidney stones. The next morning, I drove myself to the hospital, and it was confirmed. I was given pain killers and told to go home and rest. Typically, in about two days the stones would pass. This time they did not. Two days before the trip I went to my urologist, and he attempted to break up the stones, but he could not since they were lodged. He gave me more medication and was about to send me home. I shared with him that I had to leave in two days to travel back to the Third World country of Haiti. There was a meeting I could not miss. Normally, the doctor would be concerned because the stones could cause an infection if they got stuck and then tell me not to travel. This time I was shocked at his response. He replied, "It's okay. It just so happens that I will be in Port-au-Prince next week at King's Hospital doing surgeries. If you have a problem, come see me there." How incredible that God already saw fit to have my doctor in country just in case I had an issue! So, I took the medicine and the pain pills and traveled to Haiti in pain for the most difficult meeting of my life.

The meeting was set up between Daniel, Franz, and me. It was to be held at Franz's property located in the mountains outside of the city where wealthier people lived. That day James and I set out for the long trek into the hills. We left early, and a few hours later arrived at a perfectly manicured piece of property. It was clear unspoken messages were being sent that he was wealthy and had power. Laborers were all around trimming trees and bushes. After we parked and prepared to enter, James turned toward me and said, "Pastor Mike, you must be very careful here. They might be planning to do you harm. Please do not eat or drink anything they give you. I fear they are going to try and poison you." We were welcomed at the gate and then led to a patio overlooking the city. Daniel was already there talking with Franz. We were invited to sit down.

Franz explained his projects at this site, including larger dorms where an orphanage and school were said to be housed. We did not see or hear any children when we arrived, and even later it seemed empty. Franz explained that he now needed Hope Village to expand his work and that he and the supporting Nebraskan ministry wanted it returned. He also shared that all the properties legally belonged to Daniel. Once Daniel had taken possession of them, the plan was to give Hope Village to Franz and have Daniel maintain ownership of Seventy Palms. He relayed that he had heard of all the work that we put into the property and that perhaps Daniel and I could come to an agreed upon price for us to purchase it. In the middle of the discussion, Franz's wife arrived with drinks for all of us.

We were sitting in the sun, and it was hot, yet James simply let his drink sit in front of him. After a while of being caught up in the conversation and frustrated over our situation, I reached for the glass and brought it to my lips. James turned toward me and spoke volumes with his eyes. I did not ingest any of the drink and simply sat it back down and pushed it forward. The meeting lasted for hours. At one point, I reminded Daniel of our previous relationship and all that we had been through together. As he looked at me with those once bright eyes, I could see pure evil and darkness. There was no light of faith anymore. He said that he believed God had given him the property to provide for his family after years of faithful service. The discussion got more intense and ended in heated disagreement. I wanted first to talk to our lawyer, so I managed to delay any action until the next meeting.

As we returned to the vehicle, Franz and I continued to talk about Haiti while James and Daniel walked off to the side of the parking lot. Their conversation intensified. It is common for Haitians to speak loudly to each other and even yell, so I did not give it much thought until Franz said to me that he feared this would end in a brawl. We walked over, and as we did, the conversation ended. James and I returned to the pickup and left for home.

While we were at least conversing with Daniel, John K and I decided to use this advantage to check on Jehovah Orphanage's condition and the children that remained there. I called Daniel and asked him if we could visit the kids. He, believing that he still had the chance for us to enter into a working agreement, agreed. That next afternoon we walked to the property of Jehovah Orphanage. We were instantly amazed at how quickly the property had deteriorated from lack of maintenance. The bakery that had been built was no longer operating, and the machinery was ruined. The stairs leading up to the second floor were broken off and gone. The women living there now simply climbed up and down on a ladder. All the tables and chairs and supplies were gone. There were no chickens left in the pen. The few children that remained came out to greet us. It was instantly apparent that their care had also deteriorated. Only one worker remained. The children looked weak and their teeth were rotting from malnutrition. We took out some supplies and balls we had brought and played with them for a bit; all the while Daniel simply sat in the background. He was not trying to hide how both the property and the care for the children had deteriorated. It was as if he wanted us to feel sympathy in order to manipulate us into a future relationship of support. After a few hours, we left saddened by all the work spent on building this facility and how the children were bearing the brunt of all this deception and greed. I walked away frustrated about our unsafe faith.

CHAPTER SIX

*"God is up to something, or the devil
wouldn't be fighting you this hard"*

—UNKNOWN

OUR NEXT MEETING WAS PLANNED for the following day.
This time we were going to meet at a hotel restaurant in
Pétionville. They requested to meet here to view the properties
afterward. They had determined their course of action, but we
were yet unsure of ours. John and I spent the evening talking
and praying, but I still needed time to process all of it.

The next day we awoke early and this time, Joseph, James,
and I all decided to go. I had planned for our lawyer to meet
us there. We traveled half-way there, and suddenly, the pickup
started to slip gears. It was undrivable within a few minutes,
and we were stuck in the middle of a Haitian road filled with
traffic. The transmission had gone out. All I could think was,
"What else could go wrong?" We could not drive it further,

and we now needed others' help to push it out of the road. As has happened on other occasions, Haitians were willing to help. I have been in a vehicle a few times when it has broken down in Haiti. Many people visiting the country are fearful because of the high crime rate, but every time I have been in a vehicle that broke down, Haitians were willing to come to assist us in pushing the car out of traffic. This time was no different. We successfully got the truck moved and found a mechanic on a side street. It became clear that it would take most of the day to fix, but we still had to get to the meeting. So, we now had to search for another means of transportation.

We decided that James would stay with the vehicle, and Joseph and I would proceed to the meeting. We do not usually ride on tap-taps (Haitian versions of public transportation), but we had no choice. The problem was that we were now tight on time, and we had to find one that could get through traffic quickly. We decided to find a motorcycle tap-tap. We shared with the driver our destination and that we were in a hurry. Telling him we were in a hurry may not have been the wisest decision I have ever made. The driver was determined to get us there on time and earn a larger tip in the process. The motorcycle weaved in and out of traffic. Due to my height, my knees even bounced off several vehicles as we sped past them. When we arrived Daniel and Franz were already waiting there for us. We were the only ones in the restaurant. We sat down and ordered drinks.

It did not take long for the conversation to pick up where

it left off. Franz said they would like the property back, and he wanted to go and see the condition of Hope Village. He reiterated that it seemed like it would be the best for both Daniel and me to agree upon a purchase price for the land and buildings located at Seventy Palms so that we could continue operating on the site. In his opinion, this would be a win for everyone. It was about this time that our lawyer showed up. Everyone expressed their displeasure at this and said they thought we were trying to keep it out of lawyer's hands. They wanted to reach an agreement without lawyers so that no one had to spend the excess money. Daniel said that if my lawyer was present, he was not comfortable proceeding without his lawyer attending. I ignored their complaints and asked them to hand their property paperwork to my lawyer for examination. They eventually relented and gave it to him. My lawyer read it over, and much to my dismay, said it looked like it was in order. If I had as much experience as I do now in Haiti, I could have challenged it further, but for now I had to accept the lawyer's opinion.

The lawyer now attempted to lead us in a negotiation for a fair price for the property. I again did not have any funds, but I believed that I could raise a fair amount to make this go away and then secure the property. Daniel responded that the value of the property had greatly increased because of all the dwellings now on it. I argued that we built the buildings and that I would not pay extra for them. Then Daniel said that he would like three hundred thousand for the property. I responded in Creole that he was crazy if he thought I would pay that much; I would not even consider that price. The argument continued to mount and get louder as all the restaurant staff stopped and watched. After a few more minutes, it became clear that we would not come to an agreement. Neither side was willing to budge. I refused to pay anywhere near his asking price, and he was determined to get as much as he could get for it. Then Franz suggested that we determine a fair rental value until I could determine where Mission Experience could purchase or rent another site. Daniel said that he would like three thousand a month rent on the property. I refused and told him that too was outrageous. By this time, I was heated. There was no money budgeted to pay monthly rent for the property. I had nowhere to bring the children, so I was stuck in this place for now. As the talk continued around the table I prayed under my breath. I needed to determine a number that I thought we could pay each month for the foreseeable future because I did not know when we would ever be able to move. Finally, a wave of peace rolled over me and I said, "I will pay you a thousand dollars a month rent and not a dime more. Also, I will not move the children until I find a safe home for them; and while we are on the property, you are never allowed on it to jeopardize the safety of the children." After some more banter, Daniel agreed. He stood, walked behind me and extended his hand to shake. But he had been deceitful and used our love for the children to feed his greed. He waited behind me. In Haiti, because the value of respect is so high, I knew that one of the highest forms of insult was to show disrespect to someone. I refused to get up and face him, because I wanted him to know that I had lost my respect for him. So, I stood, turned away from him, and left.

Everyone agreed to meet in a few hours at Hope Village. We again got a tap-tap, but this time we took our time returning. My knees could not handle much more. When we arrived back there was no one on-site but John K and our Haitian security guard. A few hours later Franz and a partner of his showed up along with Daniel. Franz had never been on the property and Daniel had not been on it for years. We walked around, showing them the property and all that we had developed. They were impressed with the property, especially the team center and its furnishings. After we were done, we all gathered in the front courtyard. Internally, my heart was grieving for losing the property and all the previous work our teams and FHI had done to build and equip the site. Franz said that I should be thankful that we were allowed to live on this property rent free the last number of years. He said that when we left he wanted us to leave all the furnishings for the gift of allowing us to be here. At this, my grief again turned to anger. I looked at him and said we would leave the property clean but made no promise about the furnishings. We agreed that we had until April to move off the site. Then Franz threatened again that if we did not want future problems, all the furnishings needed to remain. I looked directly into his

Pastor Mike & James

Our girls

eyes and said again, "I said that we would leave this property clean and in order when we leave." Then he and Joseph got into an argument in Creole. I turned and walked away. I walked quietly around Hope Village, not believing that we now lost both sites. As their fight continued, I walked out the gates and on to the streets. I needed to get away from them and the situation. I walked the neighborhood angry, frustrated and grieving. John stayed for fear that Joseph and Franz would end up fighting.

A few hours later after all the parties had left, I walked to Seventy Palms. As I entered the gate, I could see that all the children were sitting at the top of the property at the kitchen pavilion facing the front gate. Behind them stood all the staff. I could tell what they were thinking by their long, sad faces. If I had to guess at the words, it would have been, "Pastor Mike, what is going to happen to us? Are you leaving, and if you do what will happen to us and where will we live?" They all had lost their families of origin in the past; how could I allow them to lose a second family? I was sure the staff had the same questions about their jobs and how they would provide for their families if we did not continue but I had no answer. Halfway up the property, I realized I had to gain my composure. I had to find some way not to transfer my feelings of doubt and anger to them. I stepped behind one of the cottages and walked toward an old parked bus, and I punched it in anger. Then I prayed. After a few minutes, I proceeded up the hill and started to play with the children.

The day all of this took place was Carnival in Haiti. Carnival is a national voodoo holiday supported by the government and is typically filled with parades and excessive drinking. It is not safe to be on the streets much during this day, so in the past, if we were in country we simply stayed on the properties. We never went out after dark. Joseph had approached me earlier in the day about some property a friend named Haitian John knew was available. Haitian John had told him that there was property for sale right next to the community where he lived and that we should come look at it. I listened, but in the moment, I did not pay much attention. I wanted to focus on the kids to help squash their fears.

Later that day, as the sun was setting, I was sitting on one of the cabins' front porch. On my lap sat one of our younger children falling asleep. As he rested, my inner turmoil began to increase. The events of the day sickly churned in my stomach. Joseph walked over to talk, sensing my frustration. I inquired about the conversation he had with his friend regarding the property. Then I looked up and told him that I wanted to go and see the property now. He looked at me surprised and said, "Now?" I said, "Yes, right now." It was clear that Joseph was questioning the wisdom of this idea. He did not fight it though because he sensed my inner turmoil and scrambled to arrange the trip as the sun already began to set over the horizon. He gathered James to take him, John K, and me. He then called Haitian John and arranged to pick him up so that he could direct us to the property. We loaded into the pickup and exited the gates. I did not know how far it was, but immediately upon leaving the property, it was evident by the time we would arrive, it would be dark.

Halfway there we picked up Haitian John. I immediately recognized him because he used to live in a tent community displaced after the earthquake. We had often ministered there over the last couple of years. He was a kind man who called himself the "mayor" of that tent village. We traveled for about an hour. At times it was slow going because the neighborhood streets were filled with people dancing and drinking. When we made the turn off the main road into the community where the property was located, the headlights shone on a crowd of people blaring music, drinking, and being loud. I was so frustrated by the day that I was not even contemplating the danger of our situation. As James beeped to get through, the crowd just looked at him. For a minute, I was not sure whether they were going to move or not. I do not know if they saw John K and me in the truck, but they slowly danced out of the way. We proceeded on a long, dark dirt road, which then turned right into a field of thorns. We exited the vehicle. It was already dark with truly little light from the moon. John and I walked in silence around the property. As we did, we both silently prayed. I asked God, "What if? What if we could purchase this property and build another orphanage?" There was not much to see except that it was a larger section of land than Hope Village and Seventy Palms combined. It was filled with briars and dense vegetation, which although hard to clear, indicated that the ground was better and even had topsoil. The last few years building on Seventy Palms was exhausting, always having to break through the hard rock to build. After about an hour of walking and praying, we packed up to leave. There was no huge revelation or clear direction laid upon our hearts. There was a simple question, "What if?"

We returned to Hope Village later that night. Even though the travel time was long because of all the people celebrating, we arrived without incident. John K and I were exhausted from the long emotional day, so we headed to bed. As we conversed in our dark room, John K said to me, "I am excited. God is going to use this. It is going to turn out better than we could imagine." In the moment I did not feel the same. The student was now teaching the teacher about faith.

CHAPTER SEVEN

*"Sometimes in life, you have to make a
decision and fall on your knees."*

—*THE CRUEL SEA*, NICHOLAS MONSARRAT

*"I have been driven many times upon my knees
by the overwhelming conviction that I had
nowhere else to go. My own wisdom and that of
all about me seemed insufficient for that day."*

—ABRAHAM LINCOLN

THE NEXT FEW DAYS AND WEEKS WERE a blur after I returned
to the States. I began with a random Google search on
ministries operating in the greater Port-au-Prince area. This
was followed by emails and phone calls to any that appeared
on the searches. I was looking for spiritual guidance, available
land, as well as ministries that had space available if we
needed to move and house the children. At the same time,

the Haitian staff continued with their search for property. I was set to return to Haiti within three weeks with a team of teens from Nebraska. I needed to figure out how to ensure their safety while at the same time view properties and start emptying Hope Village. All the ministries that I contacted were gracious and supportive of our plight, but no one had available space or contacts that would advance our cause.

Then God graciously led me to a ministry named "Bonswa." I searched their website and sent an email to the address listed. The chairman of the board, Canadian John, contacted me from his home in Canada. He listened to our story, and our circumstances moved him. His response was unlike the other ministries we encountered. He shared the story of his ministry and the property on which they were presently located. They had purchased a piece of property about eight miles from our present site. Eight miles does not seem like much, but on Haitian roads and in Haitian traffic, this meant an hour and a half drive. Their community was comprised of families who had been displaced after the earthquake. Most of the families living on site were housed in tents or shacks. They had built a church, and their long-term goal was to build houses for all these families. At the time, there was a full-time missionary named Mark on site. Canadian John's response to our story was, "We are not going to let the enemy win. Even if you must move your children and staff on our site, we will figure it out." His response was a healing balm to my heart. At this point in our crises, I at least needed to know there were options. At the end of the conversation, Canadian John mentioned that the property next to them was for sale. The landowner who sold them their land had more inherited property he wished to sell, and he suggested I make plans to see it. I agreed to attempt to make the time when I returned to Haiti.

Three weeks later, I returned. The plan was to view three pieces of property while spending time praying over them. The young team that would join me would share in visiting the properties as well as being the workhorses to move everything from Hope Village to Seventy Palms. This included all the supplies, beds, tools, dining room tables and chairs, air conditioners, ceiling fans, and even the kitchen sink! The children were already living at Seventy Palms in four of the six cottages. The two other cottages that were built had incomplete interiors. Doug and Stuart would soon lead teams to finish the construction so the cottages could house teams until we found and constructed our new location.

The teens who joined me on this trip were from Cornerstone Christian School in Omaha, Nebraska. It was a large team of youth and chaperones. They did not know it at their time of training, but they would serve a pivotal role in our ministry. I updated them on our story and all that we needed to accomplish during the week. They were all excited and willing to help. The first few days began the huge task of packing and moving everything. Then in the middle of the week, we went on field trips to view properties, including taking a second look at the field I had previously visited. Every evening, we would gather and share how each team member felt about each property's pros and cons. Some properties seemed to be in safer locations, but they were all much smaller than the field. The large open space was further from the city, which felt safer and had the added benefit of having fertile ground, a rare commodity in Haiti. This piece of ground was on the top of our list, but in the back of my mind, my conversation with Canadian John from Bonswa continued to spin. I sincerely appreciated his words of encouragement, and I desired to view the property that he discussed, but time was pressed.

The workdays were intense, as there was a lot to move. We did not want to draw Daniel's attention, so we disassembled furniture and packed supplies on our bus to transport them. My concern in all of this was that Daniel would contact Franz and find ways to complicate the move since he still wished to steal all our supplies. The last thing I wanted was for this to get messy with the teens in the middle of it. All the while through this, the Cornerstone group was terrific. They never complained as they worked hard and often late into the night. Each time the bus was full, we would send someone to the street to ensure there was no activity outside Daniel's property, and then we would drive the bus to Seventy Palms. By the end of the week, almost everything was moved. The last bus full was moved the night before the team left. Plans were made to hire a few neighborhood Haitian friends to help the staff move everything else during the next few weeks. We left the country with no confrontations. Our prayers for external peace during this trip were answered and accompanied by internal peace.

I returned to the U.S. to meet with the Board of Directors to determine our next steps. After some time of prayer, we decided to host a town hall meeting. We bathed the event in prayer during the preceding days. This event would be in person as well as be livestreamed over the Internet. The guests would include everyone from our supporting congregations and donors to all our previous short-term missionaries across the U.S. The night's content would include an update of our present situation and a request for prayers toward our future property decisions.

As I continued to pray about purchasing property, my heart kept coming back to the almost four acres of thorn infested field I had now visited twice. I still did not seem to have a definitive direction but knew for sure we needed to share pictures of the field at our town hall meeting as a possible future location of our orphanage. However, as I continued to pray about where to go, I could not shake the inner nagging that before we decided I needed to visit the site next to Bonswa. There seemed to be a synergy that God was creating between their ministry and our own. In my last conversation with Canadian John, I promised to pray about making more of an attempt to visit the property on my next trip in April. He promised to be online for the town hall and pray during it for God to provide a specific direction.

The last Sunday evening of March, we gathered at

Pinecrest Community Church in Parker, Colorado. This church had been faithful supporter of Mission Experience since our inception, and it was Doug and Leslie's home church. The church was full, and many attended over the Internet. I thanked everyone for coming and shared with them our updated story. I disclosed with a spirit of brokenness what the enemy was attempting to do to our ministry and all the events that led to our present situation. I laid out the plan to move forward as outlined by the Board of Directors. We had determined that we would need to raise about one hundred and fifteen thousand dollars to purchase a piece of property large enough to continue our work. The property would need to house our present ministry and make it possible to grow the orphanage in the future. The funds would cover the cost of the property, the legal paperwork to secure it, and the building of a security wall around the orphanage site. After discussing what was necessary for funding the project, I shared pictures of the field as a possible location. I told them that we had made no offer on the land, and we were still unsure if this was the right location for us. On top of that, we had no funds in the bank.

Those gathered listened with attentiveness as I began to wrap up. The meeting's goal was to inform people and enlist their prayers, and it felt like we had accomplished that task. We spent some time in prayer and then I introduced Pastor Christian from Hales Corners Lutheran Church in Hales Corners, Wisconsin. He had previously participated in our mission trips and had come in support. Earlier, he had asked to address the crowd at the end of the evening. He stood and began sharing that the church he served remained committed to our work. After a time of prayer, the staff at Hales Corners Lutheran did not feel like the work of Mission Experience in Haiti was complete. Pastor Christian had not previously shared this with me, but they had decided to take a door offering for two weeks to support our future project. They understood that every new building project needed seed money, and they felt led to provide it. I stood there amazed at this surprise gift. I opened the envelope and found a check for thirty thousand dollars. God had begun working, even before we started planning.

The next moment was just as unforgettable. Pastor Tom from Concordia Lutheran Church in Lakewood, Colorado, suggested that we not leave today until we doubled that amount in pledges. I was overwhelmed and expected none of this. I shared again that the goal of this was not to pressure people to give but to pray and seek direction. I was unprepared for a pledge drive; however, there seemed to be a common consensus that this was a moment of faith that we all did not want to miss. Stuart was present, so he came up to lead people through a time of prayer and pledges. Within another half hour, the gift of thirty thousand dollars turned into sixty-five thousand dollars. The pace at which God seemed to be moving shocked us all. I have always told people that I am not after your money, I am after your hearts; and it seems as if

We prayed over this field

Short term missionaries and the kids

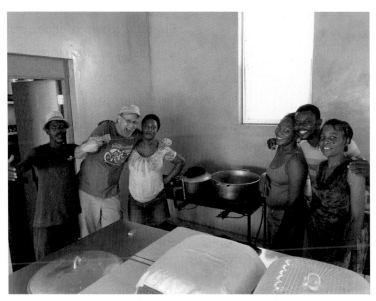

Pastor Mike and our Haitian workers

God's mission had captured them all.

The next day Canadian John from Bonswa called me to discuss the meeting. He was also amazed by all that God led to transpire. He told me that he had been online during the gathering. He had seen the pictures of the property that we were considering purchasing and once again encouraged us to not make a final decision until we viewed the property next to their community. He said that area next to Bonswa looked remarkably like the pictures I shared. I thanked him for his support and asked if he could send me photos of the field.

A few days later, I received the pictures from Canadian John of both the vacant field for sale and the Bonswa community. He was correct in that the area was similar to the field we were considering. One of the pictures included the resident American missionary on-site and a Haitian man. I looked closely at the picture, and I realized I recognized the Haitian man. As Canadian John and I continued our conversation, he shared that the man's name was John. He was the man who was previously called the mayor over a tent community near our old property that was filled with displaced people after the earthquake. Over the last few years, Mission Experience sent numerous teams into this tent city to minister and provide encouragement and hope. After more discussion, we realized that the people housed on Bonswa's property now were some of the same people we had been ministering to over the last few years. The tent community had been disbanded a year or so prior and now they found a home at Bonswa. I requested more pictures of the property from Canadian John because now my interest was piqued. I thought we had found the property we were to purchase, but maybe there was something here that had to be researched further. Maybe there was a connection that God had been creating behind the scenes for the last few years.

In the next round of photos, I recognized the church that was on their site. I could not place where I had seen it, but it all seemed so familiar. I had been there before, but I could not figure out when. Where was this place and why did it feel like Deja vu? Although I could not yet identify it, my curiosity was now intensifying. I requested that John send me the satellite coordinates; this would assist me in finding the answer. I received the coordinates from Canadian John, and my mouth dropped open. Only God could do this!

I checked and rechecked the coordinates. I sat stunned. This was too amazing. Only God could accomplish this. Some people believe in chance and explain away the parts of their lives that they cannot understand, but then there are events like this that have no natural explanation. There was a reason that the church located on the Bonswa property was so recognizable to me. The reason was that I had driven past it two times in the last few months. The land that Canadian John was so sure God wanted us to consider next to them was the very same field that I had stepped foot on and prayed over that night back in February. The Haitian man in the picture that I recognized was Haitian John, who joined us on the first trip there. The land that I felt we were being led to was the very field located right next to Bonswa! This was no coincidence. This was the hand of God.

My next trip back into Haiti was scheduled for April. By this time, the fundraising had brought in almost eighty thousand dollars. On this trip about mid-week, we loaded up the team and traveled over to the field to pray and meet the landowner. This was the first time I met Mark, the full-time Bonswa missionary. We were excited about the connection that God seemed to be creating between the two ministries. As we visited, the team got out and prayer-walked the property. By this time, the entire neighborhood had heard that we were thinking about buying the property and they all gathered around to see if a transaction would be made. I met the landowner, and it was decided that it was not a good idea discussing money in front of all these people. It was not safe for the landowner nor us. Mark, the landowner, and I went inside their church building to have a discussion. It helped that Bonswa had already purchased land from this landowner. This meant that there was an established relationship of trust already built.

After a brief discussion of the land, the conversation turned toward the price of the property. Figuring out land costs in Haiti is a little more complicated because they sell land by "carreau" and "cemtieme" instead of the acre. The field consisted of just over 3.5 acres, which is a little larger than one carreau. The landowner offered the land to us at the same price he had sold the land to Bonswa approximately three years earlier. I asked for a moment and went out to meet with Pastor Christian who was on this trip, and Steve F, a future Board of Directors member. The plan today was to visit with the landowner. We had not raised all the money that was needed, but all I could think was, "What If God was providing this land for us?" The price was fair. I did not even feel led to present a counteroffer, because I also wanted to be fair to the landowner. I did not feel like we could pass it up, and neither did Christian or Steve F. I prayed and returned to the meeting. I told the landowner that Mission Experience would purchase the land at his price. We shook hands and left. The team was excited and overjoyed by what God had done in such a short time. I was amazed at how God was taking our garment of sadness and turning it into praise. Two months earlier, we had lost everything. Now we had a new property.

I had no idea how long it would take to complete the legal paperwork, build a new orphanage, or even how much it would cost. We had to make sure that we did it correctly, so as not to allow the enemy a foothold to steal it again. All legal paperwork in Haiti is complicated, and even more so when it concerns property. The first step in Haiti is to have your property surveyed. Next, a notary works on the legal ownership paperwork and makes sure the title is clear. After this is completed, the new owner must register the property with the government and then later work on the deed. The struggle is that in Haiti, after the earthquake, many records of deeds were destroyed. Finding a deed or creating a new one is a long process in Haiti. This was going to be a long journey, but the landowner immediately called a surveyor. He arrived within an hour and began his work right away. Later that night, the team returned to Seventy Palms and celebrated God's goodness.

It took another month, but by the end of May, we stopped the fundraiser because we had raised the hundred and fifteen thousand dollars that we needed for Phase One. In this first step we needed to build the security walls needed around the orphanage for the safety of the children who live there. In June, Doug and Stuart led a team to lay the foundation of our walls. Jordany, our Haitian concrete worker, then built the walls with Haitian workers after the team left. By the end of the summer, the eight-foot-high walls were finished with a layer of razor wire on top. In the next few months, we dug a well for fresh water and started building a house for a new security worker to live on site. We now had land. We had a future. The next question was, where would we get the funds to build the buildings? Doug began the work of laying out an architectural concept for the future property. We had learned so much in Haiti over the years, and now we had a chance to resolve all our previous issues by designing our own layout and buildings. We did not want to lose the momentum, so immediately we began to share our story and drawings with all those who would listen. We did not know where the funds would come from, but God already had provided time and time again when we did not have the funds for the next step. We just needed to see whose heart God was going to touch next. It would not be long until I would receive a phone call from a man named Kenny and God opened the next door.

CHAPTER EIGHT

"After you have suffered for a little while,
the God of all grace, who called you to His
eternal glory in Christ, will Himself perfect,
confirm, strengthen and establish you."

—1 PETER 5:10

"While it looks like things are out of
control, behind the scenes there is a God
who has not surrendered authority."

—A.W. TOZER

AMID THE WILD ROLLERCOASTER RIDE OF these last five months during one of our Board of Directors meetings, Steve P said, "I have been part of churches where we felt like God was leading us, but I have never been part of anything where it seemed like God just took over." It appeared to us that God was sometimes providing before we even had a chance to pray, although every breath during these months were prayers. The walls were getting built and beauty seemed to be rising from the ashes. We had no idea how God would provide for the next steps of the build, but by now, we had learned to simply leave space for God to move and rest in Him.

Then one day, I received a call from Kenny from Colorado Springs, Colorado. He had been successful in business and was now serving God by creating and installing buildings on the mission field. Larry, one of his employees and Doug's brother who had served on a mission trip with us two years prior, shared our current situation with him. Kenny asked if I would drive to Colorado Springs and meet with him to share our story. A week later, Doug and I traveled to his residence. I did not know much about Kenny at the time, and I had no sense of what God would accomplish, so I prayed and went with an open heart. Kenny graciously welcomed us into his beautiful home. Doug and I recounted our story of loss and God's amazing provision. Our children were still living at Seventy Palms at the time, and although we had purchased new land, there was a lot of building that needed to occur before we could even consider moving them.

After we were through telling our story, Kenny shared the work that he had begun in numerous locations around the world. God had blessed his business, and he was moved to give back. He had started a small manufacturing plant where he fabricated steel structures and then shipped them to various mission locations to assemble. He had already built two large steel warehouses on the outskirts of Port-au-Prince, Haiti for another ministry. He showed us some of his photos of the structures he had constructed. We were impressed. After seeing the pictures, we shared Doug's architectural property drawings with Kenny. The largest buildings needing to be built included two dorms (designed to provide a residence for the children and the nannies), a kitchen pavilion, and a large team center to house short-term teams. Kenny was excited about all God had already accomplished in such a short time and about the possibility of working together. He looked straight at me and said that he would like to make a proposal. He pointed at the two dorms and the team center. He said, "If I donated these three buildings and bring construction teams, could you enlist additional workers to support the build and raise funds to complete the interior?" I was speechless. I looked at Doug and wondered if my eyes were as wide as his. Internally I shouted, "Yes! I have no idea how and where I will raise the money, but yes!" Outwardly, I reached out my hand in a calm manner to shake his and said, 'Yes, I agree." The next steps were discussed, and we agreed to work together. Kenny said the buildings would be designed by his architect in Colorado Springs, bearing in mind the hurricanes and storms that sweep through the Caribbean. The steel would be cut to size, and then all the buildings, including doors, windows, and supplies would be shipped to Haiti and assembled there. He also committed to covering the costs of the concrete foundation work. We were amazed. As we started to leave, he stopped us and said, "Do you have a skid steer down there? You are going to need one for all this work." Knowing the high cost of even a used skid steer, I replied, "No." He responded, "That's OK. I will purchase a used one and send it down there for you." This was incredible. There are times that you feel like you are being prompted and led by the Holy Spirit; then there are other times when God really does just take over. God moves where and when He pleases. I did not know why He was choosing to move in this way, but all we could do was hold on for the ride.

Our initial plan was to erect the frame for Dorm One and then build out the inside to temporarily house both the girls and boys on separate sides with independent bathrooms. This way, we could move the children once this first dorm and kitchen pavilion were finished and not wait until the other buildings' completion. This first dorm would also provide housing for the nannies and temporary housing for some of the other staff members and their families. Over the next few months, the trips included putting in a septic system, burying water lines, and preparing the ground to pour the first dorm foundation. Team members came from across the United States to help. They stayed in the cottages at Seventy Palms and each day would make the long trip back and forth the new property. In the evenings, after a hard day of work, everyone would shower and have dinner, and then come out to be with the children. They would play, teach, and do crafts into the night. There was not much downtime, but no team members ever complained. They came from all walks of life—

from high school and college students to seventy plus year-old team members. They came with different occupational backgrounds—from preachers to a Super Bowl winning quarterback, Mark Rypien, and his wife, Danielle. They came from every skill level—from contractors to those with no construction experience. They all worked hard, sweated a lot, and served with willing hearts.

I know that there are numerous books written today that question the value of short-term missions and the amount of money needing to be raised to fund a trip. Many of these books make some valid points. If people are going to serve with the wrong mindset or just come to experience a trip overseas, then the money could be more efficiently spent on the mission itself. Mission Experience does "mission trips" and not "experiential tourist trips." Hosting short term mission teams is indeed a lot of work for full-time missionaries and the locals who serve beside them. But if we can continue to receive missionaries with hearts like those who served during this year of intense work, Mission Experience would happily host them all year long. Most team members come hoping to change a life for the better, but there is more to missions than that. I have witnessed numerous lives changed forever by just one trip. However, this means that teams should arrive with hearts open to the possibility that their lives might be the ones changed. Team members must come willing to receive as much or more than they are willing to give.

While Doug was in country working with one of the teams

Stuart, James, and our kids

Ellie and one of our kids

Groundbreaking at God's Garden

to prepare the first dorm foundation site, the first container of supplies arrived late one fall night. The team worked with spotlights to get it safely on the property. It was very dark in the field, and the container had to be removed from the truck and placed on a level section of the property. Carefully the task was accomplished with no injuries. Everyone was excited that now all the supplies were there to assemble the first dorm. The build could begin.

In the weeks to come, the first foundation was poured and the beams started to go up. It was not long before it began to take shape. Amid all this labor, I received a phone call from another board member JK (a fourth John in our story). He had secured the funds from a Texas church to cover the building of the kitchen pavilion. Before the dorm was even complete, our Haitian concrete workers began work on the kitchen pavilion with the funds now in place. Over the next few months, Doug worked with teams to frame in the first dorm, and Stuart worked with additional team members to build and install the trusses for the roof on the kitchen pavilion. A lot was getting accomplished in a short time and we could see God's hand in all of it.

During this year, we did not hear much from Daniel. Initially, we heard rumors spreading through our old neighborhood that he sought ways to scare me into leaving Haiti. His goal was to take possession of Seventy Palms, where the kids were still living, and all our supplies stored on site. Occasionally, he would call James and attempt to elicit information from him. We were hesitant to allow him to find out where we purchased property or to have him hear how advanced we were in our project for fear that he would create more trouble. His threats eventually stopped. He was not receiving as much money as he wanted, but he was still extorting a thousand dollars a month. As the months passed, it was clear he had found others interested in the land who would pay more than us; however, our present lease was sealed through legal documents. He was stuck with us until we were ready. Surprisingly though, Daniel had a brief softhearted moment as he inquired of James once in a conversation, "Do you think that Pastor Mike still loves me?" James' simple response was, "You know Pastor Mike's heart."

While the progress was steady, and outside trouble from Daniel stopped for a time, we had our own struggles in our new community. When we arrived, many locals did not seem to be pleased about our arrival. On one of our initial trips, as we drove into the neighborhood, there was a group of men sitting on a porch. As we passed, the team members waved while one man stared at the bus and swiped his thumb threateningly across the base of his throat. He was not pleased. Bonswa was our neighbor, but there was an active voodoo community in the area as well. One day when we arrived, our security workers took us to our field in front of the orphanage walls. They showed us some iron rods which had been driven in the ground and the small area set on fire. They explained that what we were looking at was evidence of a ceremonial voodoo curse placed against us. When we moved, we did not leave spiritual warfare behind. There is a real battle going on each day that we cannot see. Whether it is perceived or not, it is there. St. Paul writes in Ephesians 6:11–12, "Put on the full armor of God, so that you can take your stand against the devil's schemes. For our struggle is not against flesh and blood, but against the rulers, against the authorities, against the powers of this dark world and against the spiritual forces of evil in the heavenly realms" (NIV). Satan had a devised plan against us, and he was still seeking to set back our ministry.

We told our workers to get rid of the rods, but they refused to touch them with their hands. They understood what evil these rods represented. Instead, one of them got a shovel and removed it. We were not going to allow this to scare us or set us back. God had provided this land, and we would love and serve this community in which He placed us. Fear was our enemy, and we would not allow it to control us. We had already hired local construction workers, some of whom were voodoo practitioners. They worked hard for us, and we were already making relationships within the community. We were determined to continue to create connections and allow space for God to transform hearts.

During all this construction work, before a trip the following summer, I received a call from one of the ministries I had previously contacted. They knew that we had found land, and they were searching for a potential property to expand their ministry in the future. They inquired if I knew of any available land. I wrote to them and told them our original landowner still had some sections available. They asked if I could view the ground and send them pictures. During the next trip, I made arrangements to meet with the landowner and visit some of his other land parcels. He came on Wednesday, and he, James, and I decided to go see three sections. Before I left, I walked into the dorm to inform the rest of the team that I would be leaving for a brief time. One of our missionaries named Ellie was there serving on her fourth trip in less than ten months. To make sure someone knew where I was going, I told her that I was going to look at these properties for another ministry.

Ellie's first trip was the previous November before all this mess had started. She was not new to short-term missions, having served previously multiple times in both Vietnam and Russia. On her first trip to Haiti, she was deeply touched by the children and decided to return on the January team. Then she came again in April on the trip when we purchased the property. It was clear that God was working on her heart, and she had a growing connection with the children. The ministry desperately needed a female on staff to work with the nannies on growth plans for each of the children, and I felt she might be the one. Previously, I had talked to the board that if God ever opens the door, we might consider hiring her for this position.

Since all the properties were within walking distance, the three of us set out on foot. The first property was right around the corner, located on the main street through our neighborhood. Its rear wall was connected to our existing property. We walked around the property, examining its condition and size, and then returned to the front. The property was about one acre in size. I inquired of the landowner how much he was asking for the property. His price was similar to what we had paid for the land we had purchased. Then I stood silently praying over the property. As I stood there looking back into the property, I had what can only be described as a vision. I saw a community of businesses. The entire field was filled with people operating businesses around the edges with customers walking between them. It was a vision of a business center where we would provide jobs for locals as well as the children as they aged out of the orphanage. It would also be a location where we could provide job training and help locals own and operate their businesses. Even though I was on this trip to find potential land for another ministry, it seemed like God moved. I turned to the landowner and told him that he could not sell this property. He looked at me surprised and asked, "Why?" I told him that Mission Experience needed it. We again did not have a dime to pay for it. I just knew we had to buy it. We agreed to the price and shook hands. We then went on to view other properties to see if they would fit the needs of the other ministry. Later that afternoon, after we returned to our property, I walked into the dorm and saw Ellie. I told her I had an announcement for the team. She looked at me with a broad grin and said, "You just bought more property, didn't you?" I smiled. The team assembled and

I shared the new component of our vision. Once again, we marveled at how much bigger God's plan was than our own. We prayed and thanked God for His goodness.

CHAPTER NINE

"To be a Christian without prayer is no more possible than to be alive without breathing"

—MARTIN LUTHER

BY SEPTEMBER OF 2017, THE DORM was moving toward completion. The interior was almost finished, with only some of the plumbing and electrical remaining. Daniel kept calling James, asking when we were moving. Since we did not want any more problems, it was growing in importance to get our children moved into a more permanent and secure location. Two teams were scheduled for that month. The first team would finish as much of the final projects as possible, while the second team would attempt to finish any uncompleted tasks and decorate the rooms and move in the children. The Mission Experience staff was planning on staying both weeks because we needed both trips to be successful. The greatest concern was the amount of work still to be done.

The first team was blessed with essential workers, which included a plumber and an electrician. It got ridiculously hot in the large steel building now split into rooms during the day, making intermittent breaks a necessity. Each break, the team would come out soaked in sweat. As we entered mid-week, the list of tasks to be completed was still extensive, and some on the team had questions about whether we would get enough completed to move the children. By this time, my patience with Daniel and Seventy Palms was wearing thin. It seemed like everything was breaking there. The electricity kept having issues, and we were just patching things together to keep it operating until we could move out. Seventy Palms was being held together by prayer.

The work at "God's Garden" continued. This was the name we selected for the new property. We took months praying about the name, and as soon as Stuart suggested it, it seemed to stick. It was a gift from God, and we believed that God would raise the children as a "crop" of His faithfulness. We also thought that God would have a harvest of souls for His kingdom from this voodoo infested neighborhood. We knew it would mean years of work, but we have always rested in God's faithfulness.

While working on the first dorm, Kenny sent down a worker with the first team to prepare the ground for the foundation of the second dorm and lay the rebar. The hope was that one of our volunteers flying in mid-week could provide some assistance. We would not get to building dorm two for another few years, but Kenny pushed to get his part complete. The concrete pour was scheduled for the end of the week, so time was of the essence. As our work continued, so did the work of the enemy. Tensions rose with the heat, but we could not allow him to get us sidetracked nor succeed in his attempt to create a spirit of division. If the enemy cannot succeed in frontal assaults, he will try internal division. Disciples of Jesus must constantly be aware of the areas in which they are vulnerable. I often ask people in team training where they are susceptible to attacks. I tell them that if they do not know, then they should ask themselves this question, "If I were the enemy, where would I attack me?" As tensions arose, I would often catch the team members praying for the unity of staff, the clarity of the detail work, and accomplishing the tasks before us. Mission trips have a way of expanding your prayer life. We determined that nothing was going to hinder the work that we were called to do. So, in faith, we all kept moving forward. The dorm was almost complete, and the kitchen pavilion was close enough to completion that it was usable.

While all this was happening, Hurricane Irma was forming in the Caribbean and headed for Haiti. It was a Category Five hurricane that forecasters were predicting to change to a Category Four upon landfall. Each time we had a break, a team member would check on the storm's location and its projected path. Landfall in Haiti was predicted for mid-week. The team was determined to keep making the trip each day to work at the site, but they were concerned that the storm would make it difficult to leave. Those at home still planning to come were worried whether they should even attempt to make the trip. We prayed, and we worked.

Hurricane Irma hit the Leeward Islands on September 6, 2017, with sustained winds of 180 miles per hour. It was recorded that Antiqua and Barbuda were hardly left inhabitable. On September 7[th,] it hit the northern part of Haiti and the Dominican Republic as a Category Five hurricane with over 15 inches of rain. Although Haiti's loss was not as devastating as other islands, the loss of crops, clean water, electricity, and housing caused more suffering on this impoverished nation. Each time we had a break, the team turned on the radio to listen to the predictions about the storm. We prayed for those affected. Concern mounted for many team members hoping to leave as scheduled in a few days. Within twenty-four hours, all those planning on arriving in the second team canceled. Hope that we would get the opportunity to move the children on this trip was fading. As the storm passed over us, there was little local damage and no damage at the Haitian airport. With that, our confidence grew that our team members would be able to leave and find an airport open in the US. But then there was a surprising twist. The hurricane was back at sea, heading straight for the southeastern United States. At first, we were not worried because Florida and the southeast have experienced storms like this previously. We assumed that they would be able to handle the impact of the storm, but then Hurricane Irma started gaining momentum again at sea.

Members of the team scheduled to leave soon became increasingly worried about the storm's effects on airports. Two of the members had critical work engagements, so they decided to leave early. They got their flights changed and left. The number of flights into Florida was already decreasing, but they were able to find a flight into JFK in New York City. Additional team members were starting to wonder about their flights and began to contact their travel agents. Hurricane Irma swept over part of Cuba and then headed to the southeastern United States. Later, it would be documented as the most powerful Atlantic hurricane in recorded history. On September 10th Hurricane Irma hit Florida. Later it would be reported that as many as 1.5 million people would lose power from Florida as far inland as Georgia. Six and a half million people had to evacuate their homes. Airports from Florida to Georgia were shut down due to flooding and power issues. All flights to the US were canceled, and no one else could leave. The remaining team members scrambled to make arrangements with their families and employers back home to cover their extended leave of absence. It seemed that God had just allowed their trip to be lengthened. In Haiti, the rains were over, and the sun returned, so we got back to work.

Most of the team ended up staying an additional four days. The more extended stay was an inconvenience for many of them, but I saw it as God's hand of provision for

Regina (Stuart's wife) and our children

Move-in day at God's Garden

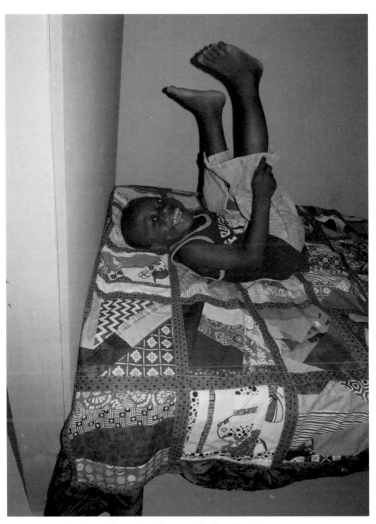

Move-in day at God's Garden

Short term missionaries & the kids worshipping

Pastor Mike and one of our boys

us. We now had the workforce we needed. We continued to work hard as we realized that our opportunity to move the children could be soon. The electricity was completed as well as most of the plumbing in the dorm. After four days some of the missionaries started to leave, while the staff and a few remaining missionaries prepared for the move. We were finally on the verge of leaving our past behind us.

But a nagging question rang through my heart, "How do we move all the children and supplies without Daniel and others finding out?" The plan was not to notify him until after we were moved entirely, and the kids were safe. Seventy Palms was located a block from his property, and we had to pass by it to leave the neighborhood. It was clear we were going to need the protection of God. I prayed that the move would be smooth, and God would cover Daniel's eyes, allowing our activity to be silent and peaceful.

We began preparing the kids for the move. Our numbers had expanded now to 23 kids, so it was complicated. We told them they needed to pack up everything they owned–which was not much–and assist in packing all the kitchen supplies, food, and bedding. Yes, we once again took everything, including the kitchen sinks! We did not move any shelving or bed frames this time because we built bunk beds attached to the walls at God's Garden. We planned for two children to live in each cubicle. For the first time in their lives, they would have their own space. Each would have their bed and even a shelf where they could display what they owned. Also, they would no longer have to share one toilet and shower because now they had three of each along with four bathroom sinks on each side of the dorm. As the staff and children packed, our problems with the electricity at Seventy Palms continued. We kept patching it together as our power was diminishing. We needed it to last just a few more days. Two days before we left, the well pump died, and we could no longer pump water. This left us only with the water that was in our holding tank. This close to leaving we decided not to fix it because we needed all our attention on the move.

The day finally arrived. It was Tuesday September 12th, 2017. The kids worked hard getting everything packed while the team members worked on decorating rooms in the new dorm. Earlier that day we loaded all their mattresses into the bus and delivered them to God's Garden. The team had new sheets for each bed and a thin quilt made by amazing quilters in the U.S. We had already disassembled the kitchen at the old property and reassembled it at God's Garden. We left the old picnic tables and made new tables. As the team worked, James, Kerby, and I took the bus to move the children and staff. It was already getting late, but everyone was excited about what was about to happen.

When we got back to Seventy Palms, it was already early evening. The kids were energized and excited. You could feel the joy and electricity in the air. Some of the older kids had joined us on a trip or two to God's Garden over the last twelve months to assist with the build, but most of the children had never been there. Kerby was now old enough that he worked with the teams regularly. All the kids knew was that they were moving to a new home where they would be safe. The children filled the bus with everything they owned. They knew they would never be back. The staff was just as excited and assisted in loading the remaining supplies. Finally, as the sun started to go down, we all got on the bus. The time to move had arrived. All we had to do was get everyone safely past Daniel's property. I tried to keep the kids calm so that we would not make a scene as we left. All the suitcases and supplies were out of sight on the floor of the bus. Even if Daniel noticed, I wanted it to seem like we might just be taking the kids out for dinner.

We drove the bus to the gate. Then our security guard opened the gate, and we headed out. Much to our surprise, our exit would be anything but quiet. As the bus pulled out, the neighboring Haitian families and children lined both sides of the street. Our relationship had grown with these families over the last years as many of their children often came to the orphanage to play. As we drove through the crowd, they clapped, jumped up and down, and yelled. They were saying goodbye and thanking us. The quiet exit we planned became a loud celebration. It no longer mattered that we were still in Daniel's neighborhood. What mattered was the joy on our kids' faces and their smiles that beamed ear to ear as they hung out the windows waving goodbye to their friends. I had no idea they knew we were leaving, but it was humbling to see how much our presence meant to the people of the neighborhood. I waved goodbye as a tear rolled down my cheek.

We arrived at God's Garden about an hour later. The sun had gone down, and it was now dark. The kids were wired with excitement, but so were we and the staff. We turned into our new neighborhood and drove up to the gate of our God's Garden. As the gate opened, the children and adults were leaning out the windows, trying to get a glimpse of their new home. Leslie and Doug and missionaries Rebecca, Suzanne, Kailee, and Ellie were there with smiling faces waiting to greet them. The kids ran off the bus and into their waiting arms. We unloaded the bus in front of the dorm and gathered all the kids together. We told them that their rooms were ready, and their names were on their new beds. We prayed and let them loose. They ran with anticipation into the dorm. They found their bed, and many jumped up and down on it. Their eyes got large as they looked at the small items that already filled their shelves. They ran into the bathroom and turned all the showers on and off and flushed the toilets repeatedly. They gave long hugs to the missionaries. Three of the boys came up to me and held on with bright, brilliant smiles and just said over and over "Thank you, Pastor Mike, thank you." All our hearts melted, and the exhaustion from weeks and hours of hard work did not matter any longer. We gathered the children to pray and bless their new home together. Then we sat out in the dark on the ground and ate cake to celebrate.

Later that night, the team returned to a dark empty

Seventy Palms. The next day we all would be leaving. The property was now eerily silent. The only water that remained was in the holding tank, and there was not much left. There would not be any showers. The few items like the generator that remained would be brought over later by James and some hired Haitians. The air conditioning in the girl's cottage did not work, so we gathered the few remaining fans to create at least air movement so that the girls could get some rest. We sat in the dark on the property, allowing the events to sink in.

God, as always, had been good and faithful. We had worked hard to make this property livable, but it no longer was our home. I reflected on when I first accepted this challenge. At that time, I figured, with God's help, we could manage this small orphanage and possibly expand the number of children from thirteen to twenty. Perhaps this is just what God wanted me to think. I thought it was manageable, but then came the heartache; yet through it all, I never felt released from this call. We had already exceeded that number of children, and when the second dorm was complete, we would be able to house up to sixty children. Also, with all the extra land, the possibilities were endless. The ministry went through hell, but God had a plan all along, even when we could not see it. There are times I think that God only shows us what we can handle and manage so we do not get overwhelmed. I would never have imagined all the doors God had begun to open. My heart was already dreaming of the possibilities.

When we awoke the next day and packed the bus to leave,

the team was quiet. The last two weeks had a great ending, but it had been an emotional roller coaster. All our bodies were beginning to crash. Finally, we boarded the bus for the last time on this property. I went back to turn off all the lights and fans. I found the switches in the on position, but the lights and fans were already off. The power was dead. The electrical system on the property had shut down even though the generator was still running. I had the inner feeling that it was symbolic, that the Holy Spirit had left the property. We drove to the airport in silence, reflecting on the week, and returned to the U.S.

CHAPTER TEN

*"Since God is a missionary God, God's
people are missionary people"*

—EDDY HO

AFTER THE LAST YEAR AND HALF OF work, sweat, and prayer, our kids were finally moved safely to God's Garden. Their joy and enthusiasm filled our hearts, but the work was not yet done. God had expanded our vision to reach more children and provide hope and the Gospel to the community where we now lived. We celebrated God's goodness, but the spiritual battle was not over. It would just take new forms. The next step in our construction process was the team center.

Doug designed our team center based on all the lessons we had learned over the years. At this point, our property had an interior wall and gate dividing the orphanage from the future team facility and staff housing so that it could be separate from the children's housing. This also provided an additional layer of protection for our kids because all our tools and supplies were stored on the team side. Kenny and his team traveled down several times over the next months to pour the team center foundation and work with our volunteers to install the frame and roof. It was a large project. The interior included plans for four large bedrooms to house eight missionaries each. The dorm also had two staff bedrooms, a large meeting area, a kitchen, and plenty of storage space. We again faced the need for God to provide funding for the building. One thing we have learned on the mission field is the absolute reliance on God. Money never seems to be on hand when we start a project, but we pray and then step forward in faith.

God laid a burden for the team center on the heart of one of our board members. John K had come on his first mission trip with us almost two years before, but as God does so often, we watched him transform from having the heart of a volunteer into the heart of a missionary. He felt led to approach his business associates to raise funds necessary to build the team center. This opened a whole new avenue of fundraising for us in the business realm. This validated a lesson we have learned over the years to share our story with everyone because you never know through whom God will provide. God, at times, prompts the most unlikely hearts to serve and give. Our call is to have the courage to tell the story.

During the next year, teams continued to come and serve. Now that we were not in a rush to get a building completed, teams were often divided between construction, ministry to our kids, and outreach. Some worked on the team center, while others built a playground. Vacation Bible School was planned for our kids and the neighboring community children, as well as a teachers' conference for the local teachers. Some teams even had the chance to minister tent to tent in the neighboring Bonswa community. We were all relieved not to have to live each day with a fear that trouble could arise from Daniel. Since the team center was still in process, the teams stayed at a local hotel five miles away. The hotel provided meals and even a pool for relaxing in the evenings. Sometimes our groups were large enough to rent out the whole place. Often on Sunday afternoons, we would pay for the hotel to make dinner for all the team, the kids, and our Haitian staff. Then we could all spend the afternoon at the pool watching the kids laugh and play. This was a respite for us, but it also provided additional income for the owner and the employees of the hotel. Over the years, our sensitivity to building up and supporting the local economy intensified into a core principle for our ministry.

When we first started serving in Haiti, much of our supplies and labor came from the U.S. The more we matured in ministry, it became clear that we had to build up and support the local economy to help our children be leaders in their own country. Up to this point, we had shipped in our tools and supplies in trailers. We did not know it, but we had been undermining the local businesses. Now we purchased everything we could in-country and made strategic relationships with business owners. We have even hired two local ladies to start a business making Haitian peanut butter called "mamba" to supply us monthly. We now purchase almost all food in the country and even enjoy more fresh fruit of the Caribbean from local markets. We have learned that any ministry serving in a foreign country should make their ministry as radically local as possible. It provides jobs, builds relationships, and supports the local economy.

A strong local economy will also support future jobs for our children. One of the reasons our ministry has been supported and encouraged by Haitian government officials is that we decided in the beginning not to adopt our children out. We have chosen to raise them in Haiti so that they could take their faith, knowledge, and skills to affect change in their own culture for the long term. In the past, every book I have read about ministry to orphans in foreign countries has suggested adoption. I do support adoption and admire many programs serving in this fashion. There are times that children must be moved for their survival. The struggle with adoption is that when you adopt out people come and select the best and brightest children and remove them from their culture. I call it cherry-picking. We have chosen to raise, educate, and provide a means for these children of faith to remain and positively influence Haiti.

The following spring while back in the U.S., I received a phone call from a friend in Greeley, Colorado. A year before, I had helped pray at her home when her family was experiencing some unexplainable issues. Spiritual warfare does not just happen overseas. She had called to relay a message from a mutual acquaintance from Ohio who urged her to share the concern with me. He felt this was from God and was extremely specific. To be honest, when someone uses the rhetoric that they have a "word from the Lord," I, along with many others, become skeptical. It is partially due to my theological training and my background, but also because of experience. I have been a pastor long enough to have heard people tell me that God told them something that was nothing more than a verbal drape over their agenda. The interesting thing here was that this message had no personal agenda. This mutual friend said, "Please let Pastor Mike know of this danger. In the future, a stranger is going to offer him a ride. He must not take it, because it could cost him his life."

Ok, I will admit that this got my attention. He then added that I would know it was happening because I would feel my stomach flip at their invitation. Upon consideration, I thought, "When is the last time that I had taken a ride with a stranger who offered?" I could not immediately think of one. The only strangers I had ridden with over the years were taxi and shuttle drivers, but I asked them for a ride and not the reverse. I assumed that if there was any truth to this word, it must pertain to Haiti, but my return was not for a few months. At this time, I was home building teams and fundraising, so I just informed the board, and they committed to be in prayer over the issue. In the meantime, while I continued to pray for discernment, the ministry needed to continue.

In the Book of Ephesians, it reads, "We wrestle not against flesh and blood" (Eph. 5:17, ESV). After those words, St. Paul lists the different powers that set themselves up against us. The term "wrestle" carries with it the connotation of hand-to-hand combat. With all my years sparring in martial arts, I have an appreciation for this concept. Often when you ground fight, it is like a chess match. Your opponent makes a move and then you respond. One of the most impressionable exercises we had done over the years in the gym was when we put a chessboard in the middle of the floor as we worked out. We would run through a series of exercises and now and then return to the chessboard to play our next move. We were learning to think strategically while exhausted. There are times in life and ministry that the war feels like a personal chess match where you never underestimate the enemy or the strategy he is using. We need to always be observant while resting in the truth of Scripture. We are in the middle of a battle. The battle is the Lord's and not ours. We are fighting a defeated enemy because of the victory won through the death and resurrection of Jesus, but we are not to let our guard down, as I have learned in Haiti.

The work on the team center continued through the summer months. The interior walls were going up and the large task of running the electrical had begun. It was again exciting to watch the progress we were making. The summer months are typically slow for us. It is just too hot in July and August to get a lot of people excited about traveling to Haiti. This is when we prefer teams providing programs for our children and the neighborhood. It is such a joy to see our kids and neighbors respond lovingly to the teams that came to serve them. Our prayer is that by their presence our Haitian friends would be reminded that God had not forgotten them. There is a time when missionary work is simply the ministry of presence.

At the end of the summer, I traveled with a new team of missionaries back to Haiti. The message from my friend remained a concern but not an active fear. I simply was not sure what to do with the information other than remain vigilantly watchful. The board and my prayer warriors were praying, but I did not share the concern with the overall team. We arrived in Haiti in the heat of September, which many times is just an extension of the August warmth. As always, we were greeted at the airport with the smiling faces of James, and our security guard, Casimir. The team and Reggie, the luggage worker who always met us at the airport, loaded the bus and headed to God's Garden. We typically go there first to greet the kids and later disembark at the hotel. Each time a team arrives they are welcomed with the joy and happiness of our children as the kids run up to each person for a hug and love. It is always a beautiful sight. Since so many of our missionaries come on multiple trips, the kids are still excited to see who returned and what new friends came. There is an ongoing discussion between missionaries about how teams

Kailee with Kerby

Our amazing Haitian nannies

Dieuslande, Mirlanda, and some of our girls

coming and going affect children and whether it creates an attachment disorder. This is a real concern for all of us, and we have had to struggle with this over the years. The blessing for our kids is that many missionaries return and some regularly enough to simply feel like an extended family. We try to keep life as normal as possible for them.

The week started ordinarily enough. The next morning we arrived from the hotel ready and excited to get to work and spend time with the children. The schedule on many of our trips is to work in the morning while the children are in school and then release part of the team in the afternoon to do a program with our kids. This is typical unless the team has been designed to run a conference or do outreach. Then around 4:00 PM, all workers stop whatever they are doing to play with the kids. We take off Sundays for rest and worship. In the evenings, we slow down, do devotions and process the day, and sometimes return to the orphanage to play games and celebrate birthdays. On some trips when it is safe, we will even take a team on a field trip to visit other ministries or experience the culture. However, on this trip, the first day was full, and we returned to the hotel late for dinner and rest.

The second day began with a Haitian breakfast of fresh fruit and juice which is always a treat. Then we had devotions and loaded the bus and made our trip through the neighborhoods to our property. As we turned the corner to the main road, we were already beginning to experience the effect of our presence in our community. When we came to the community there were no greetings to our bus from neighbors and even some perceived threats, but not anymore. Now when our bus drove down the street, people smiled and waved. Local children laughed and waved. Even when we went past the cottage where the men previously gestured a threat, their actions now turned to smiles as they greeted us. We arrived at God's Garden and parked the bus just outside of our gates. The team unloaded and went right to work. James and I stood next to the bus, talking. As we did, I saw a man come around the corner on a motorcycle.

During the past number of months, I had been searching for a new bus for our ministry. I had looked for one in Haiti and the U.S. Just before this trip, a couple of our supporters had read our request in our newsletter and purchased a bus for us. As James and I stood talking to the stranger, he inquired if we had any interest in buying a bus. Neither James nor I had ever seen this man before. He shared pictures of a bus he had for sale. He said that this bus was in Miami and needed to be shipped here, but he told us he had a similar one parked on his property if I wanted to check it out. He said if James and I got on the motorcycle with him, he would take us there. As he spoke, I heard the words of my friend replayed in my mind, "A stranger would offer you a ride. Do not take it because it could mean your life." As I looked at him, my stomach flipped. I declined and the driver drove off. In all the years I have worked in Haiti, I have never had a stranger offer me a ride. The truth is, though, if I did not recently have a bus donated, I might have been interested enough to go. Was this the offer for a ride that I had been warned about? In truth I will probably never know, but serving in such a spiritual place as Haiti, every perceived threat must be taken seriously.

In the months to come we were able to finish up the team center, and by the following summer bring two teams that would have a lasting impact on our ministry. The first one was some of the donors who came to serve and dedicate the new Fenimore Team Center. They were the first ones to spend a night in the dorm. It was a blessing to both see the completion of another part of our vision and have such generous people not only donate but also come and serve. This team also brought our first dentist. The dentist performed oral exams on all our children and provided classes on dental care. Dental care is very sparse in Haiti and non-existent anywhere near our community. It was becoming clear to us that our ministry would need to eventually expand beyond our orphanage to address the needs of our community.

The second team overlapped the following week to provide our first Vacation Bible School (VBS) for the community children. We knew that our community had a strong voodoo presence, so we were not sure how many children would attend. We prepared our field right outside the gates covering part of it with a huge blue tarp to provide shade. The team was large and filled with college students. They were excited about the potential of this outreach. To draw children, we also planned to provide lunch for all those who attended. We arranged for one hundred and fifty children and believed that would probably be on the high side.

On the first day of VBS as we started, we only had twenty-five children. It was about one child per adult volunteer. It was much less than anticipated, but we moved forward. Within an hour, the number had grown to fifty children. The momentum was starting to swell, and by the end of day one, we had just under one hundred children. The original plan was to provide a hot meal of rice and beans cooked by a hired local. When we saw we were running low, we gathered as much food as possible by splitting up the large portions and scraping every bit of food from the bottom of the pots. It became clear that the task was too big for one person, so we came up with a new plan for day two. The next day we bought a lot of Haitian bread, and part of the team started making peanut butter sandwiches in the morning while the rest of the group went to teach. The problem was that every time someone returned with the number of children, we needed extra food for the increasing numbers.

Each day the number of children grew. The crowd expanded to around three hundred by the end of the week. We had to move the VBS from our property to the church at Bonswa. We did this for the sake of capacity, but the added blessing was that we now had parents standing outside the church. This meant that even more people were hearing of the love of the one true God. Each day was filled with songs, crafts, and teaching the good news of grace in Jesus Christ. For some in this crowd, it was the first time they had heard a clear presentation of the Gospel of Christ. Food was a struggle each day. We simply never seemed to have as much as we wanted and were continually praying that God would stretch our supply further, but VBS was more of a success than we could ever have imagined.

We wrapped up the week at the hotel pool again. This time, however, would be different. We taught our children about Baptism again, and we decided to have a Baptism service at the pool. We all witnessed the grace and love of God, as sixteen children were baptized in the Christian faith. At the end of the service one of our construction workers, T-James, approached me. Up to this point, T-James was always a committed, practicing voodooist. Months before, at a Bible study for our workers, he made it clear that he had no desire to be a Christian and wanted to continue in his voodoo practices. But on this day, he swam up to me as I started to exit the pool. He said, "Pastor Mike, I want to be baptized a Christian." I told him we would love to baptize him, but he could not be a Jesus follower and still practice voodoo. He said that he understood that and repeated his request. Pastor Christian from Wisconsin was again on this team serving, so I asked him to please do the honor of baptizing T-James. He climbed back down into the pool, and we witnessed the death and resurrection of T-James in the waters of Baptism.

This extended trip had brought the usual progress and challenges we were getting used to while ministering in Haiti.

But it also held a mighty display of a redeeming God pursuing His children. Both teams left with hearts filled with blessings and memories to last a lifetime.

CHAPTER ELEVEN

"God uses men who are weak and
feeble enough to lean on Him"

—HUDSON TAYLOR

THE ONE ATTRIBUTE THAT I DISCUSS WITH all short-term mission teams is adapting and being flexible. Ministry in Haiti is complex. There are numerous variables frequently coming into play. The first one is the political climate. The political stability of this country is often in doubt. Haiti is filled with loving people, but they are not politically stable, and one could argue that they have never been. Presently, President Jovenel Moïse is not popular, and there is a lot of skepticism about his ability to lead after the Petro Caribe Scandal.[2] This political instability has resulted in demonstrations and uprisings against the President. We can track some of these potential hot spots on social forums for our safety in traveling, but others can arise in a flash and become dangerous quickly.

The second variable is the weather. Haiti is located on the island of Hispaniola, which is vulnerable to severe tropical storms and hurricanes such as the one that hit us on our September trip in 2017. Most times, these storms originate far enough out to sea off the coast of Africa which allows for some preparation, but the severity and intensity may not be known until the storm strikes land. Of course, there is always the possibility of another destructive earthquake. The Mission Experience board decided that now that our Haitian family was safely moved to God's Garden, we needed to address the variables and discuss ways to advance our ministry and make the property self-sufficient in the event another crisis arises. If there ever comes a time when no one can go in or out, we wanted the kids and staff to survive until the circumstances improve.

The first issue we addressed was to create a growth plan for each child. This caused us to return to the discussion of needing a staff person to get this accomplished. It is fine to provide a safe, faith-based learning environment for our children to live and grow, but we needed to transition them into adulthood successfully. To do this, Mission Experience hired Ellie to come on staff and fill the need of creating a life plan for each student. Ellie's heart for our orphans became apparent very quickly in her volunteer time with us. She naturally drew the children to herself. She now works closely with our Haitian staff to understand each child's needs, evaluate their giftedness, track their education, and determine how we can assist each student to succeed. She is an advocate for our students and their needs and works closely with our staff and teachers.

This all led to our first student graduation. In February of 2018, Kerby was the first graduate of our program. I had known Kerby for over eight years at this point. He had grown from a shy, little boy into a kind, young man. Like many Haitian children, his education level was behind, and it was further delayed because of the years outside the orphanage. He had a desire to learn and works hard on his schoolwork. Over the years, Kerby has become like a son to me. We talk often and he has become an ambassador for our program. Although he was over eighteen, he was taking advantage of our pledge to keep paying for school even after eighteen years of age as long as the student is passing. Now that Kerby was in his twenties, it was time to make a transition. He had always worked with teams when they came and completed chores for the orphanage, but it was time for more responsibility. On the February trip, we had a chance to celebrate Kerby and hold an orphanage graduation ceremony for him. We provided a cap for him and had him walk between all the staff, students, and missionaries to receive a graduation diploma. He was so overwhelmed that as I put my arm around him to announce what we were doing; he buried his head in my arm and wept. Then we surprised him by offering him the resident director's position of the care of the boy's dorm. This is serving as a dorm "dad." Once the second dorm is complete, he will move into an apartment there and mentor and oversee the boys. It was clear that the right decision was made when afterward Kerby sat on the picnic table bench with his head buried, still overwhelmed with emotions, and as he did, James and the thirteen younger boys gathered around him. They laid hands on him and began to pray over him. It was humbling to watch the younger boys minister to Kerby. All our hearts melted as we watched the Holy Spirit display the fruit of not only our work but the Haitian staff who serve so faithfully.

As we celebrated inside the walls of the orphanage, outside the nation again was falling into turmoil. Each day we would track what was happening in and around Port-au-Prince. As I walked around the orphanage, our Haitian workers always had the local news on their radios. The country was falling into chaos as the people rebelled against the government. The demonstrations were escalating and becoming more dangerous. Foreigners began to leave the country. Even so, we continued to minister to our children and our neighborhood. Outside the roads were being blocked, and violence was increasing. As we followed the news and the events, we heard of missionaries being evacuated from the country. Kenny, now working north of Port-au Prince with another group, contracted helicopter pilots to fly them to the airport because the main road north toward Gonaïves was blocked by a temporary concrete block wall built by the frustrated citizens. The goal of the demonstrators was to cut off Port-au-Prince from the rest of the country. At many other intersections in the city, protestors drug out semi-trailers to block roads and extort money to pass. The events were deeply troublesome, but we decided not to change our flight plans and monitor the events since we were only eight miles from the airport. At the worst, our field located in the front part of our property would allow space for a helicopter to land and evacuate us.

The final day of our trip arrived. I prepped the team for our plan to travel to the airport. Each member had contacted their prayer partners stateside, so we knew we had hundreds of people praying for us. All our male staff were going to ride with us, and we hired three officers to escort us to the airport. The police arrived early in the morning wearing riot gear and carrying semi-automatic rifles. We had planned to leave early in an attempt to get to the airport before the demonstrators got active. James and I went out to greet them and determine a route. We had to be flexible because demonstrations could arise quickly, and threat levels could change in a flash. The team boarded the bus and the police got in the lead car. We had no disruption exiting our neighborhood nor getting out to the main route; however, once we were out, we could see the evidence of the revolt against the government. In all my years of ministering in Haiti, I had never witnessed anything like it. It looked like a war zone. Trailers, piles of rocks, and concrete blocks were in the streets blocking the roadways. There were even thick black ropes tied from tree to tree at the first major intersection, blocking the roads leaving only a small space for a single car to pass through. Remnants of charred tires could

God's Garden 2019

*Doug, Leslie, Ellie, our Haitian
construction workers, and staff.*

Kerby and some of the kids having fun with music

The twins

be seen everywhere, and the air was still thick with the scent of burnt rubber. Since it was early, there were no crowds at this intersection yet, but a single man was standing a hundred yards away blocking the only path for us to cross. The police car arrived first at his blockade with their guns extended out the window. The man clearly did not want any problem with them, so he stepped aside and waved them through. After they passed, he then stepped back out in front of the bus. Before he could cause a problem, the police car circled back around and told the man that the bus was with them. He stepped aside. We continued to drive, and it was evident by the large group of people beginning to gather that up ahead a demonstration was already starting. James beeped the horn at the cops and pointed down an alleyway. James knows these streets better than anyone. They followed his suggestion. After a few more miles, we arrived at a small barricade lying across the street on fire. We slowed and the police led us through. As they drove over the rubble, some of the brush on fire got caught on their tailpipe. Once our bus made it through, the police and some locals extracted the burning bush from under their car. Then we continued toward the airport. Other vehicles, assuming it was safer with a police escort, joined in the procession behind us. There was even a United Nations vehicle among them. We drove quickly through the streets and finally arrived at the airport. We exited the bus and hugged James and our staff. I approached the lead officer to shake his hand and thank him for his help. He leaned over his semi-automatic rifle and hugged me. It was the first time I have ever hugged someone with a semi-automatic machine gun between us. He thanked us for helping the Haitian children and caring about the people. I told him that I would be back soon.

Leaving at a time of crisis creates inner conflict for any missionary. You never want to be seen as abandoning the locals when times get hard. This can cause doubt in their minds about your call and commitment. Perhaps this is why we did not leave earlier. Thankfully, our staff has never looked at us this way. We have walked together through some difficult times, and they have come to realize our role with them was more than about building an orphanage. They indeed are our family, and they know we always will return.

Key relationships with leaders in the country are vital. In modern missional books, authors challenge churches to make key relationships with community leaders, so they can address the needs of the communities in which God has placed them. It is just as crucial for the work of missionaries. Our newfound relationship with the police has been beneficial. The lead officer now comes out to God's Garden regularly to check on things. Last year on one of my trips while James and I were traveling in the city to do business, we arrived at an intersection where he was directing traffic. He noticed James and called out to him. When he found out I too was in the car, he stopped traffic in all four directions just so that he could greet us. This was also the same officer that would refer our next three children to us.

In May, James was again driving in the city when he came upon this officer. He was working on a case with three poor children. Their father had just been shot, and their mother could no longer care for them. He asked James to contact me to see if we could help. The family was living in a shack about 8' x 10' in size. They had no running water and slept on nothing but dirt floors. This is not that uncommon in Haiti, but the mother could no longer provide for the children and they were starving. There were two-year-old twins and an older brother. We were able to work with the mother and accept the children into our care. Some of our children have living relatives, while others are true orphans. Mission Experience strives to learn each of our kid's stories and encourages families to stay connected. This allows for the mother to keep in touch and even visit the children. When we celebrated the boy's birthday later that year, James asked him what he would do with the few dollars given to him as a gift. Most of the children save it to buy a special treat in the marketplace, but this little boy said that he would give it to his mom to help her. These kinds of moments remind us that God is continuously at work in the hearts of our children.

The events such as the demonstrations now made self-sustainability a high priority at God's Garden. We worked hard over the last few years to ensure that the staff and children at God's Garden can maintain a safe, productive way of life if a crisis event happens. By this time, the property already had its well to produce water and a generator to power all the buildings, but we needed to address other needs. Stuart was able to secure a family grant out of Nebraska for solar power for our property. Over the last two years, he has studied solar and become our resident expert. He and several teams have installed enough solar to power the entire property. Then in January of 2020, Doug and the Meinert mission team (a group that travels annually with us) built a chicken area with coops to raise both hens for eggs and roasters. They also rebuilt the garden and are creating a drip system. This team was able to address an even bigger issue for us with a creative solution. The bus that was donated arrived in Haiti about a year before. It was a large school bus that we were having difficulty driving through the narrow streets of Haiti. On this January team, was a missionary who worked on custom cars, so he cut the bus in half, removed a seven-foot section, and welded it back together. It was creativity on the mission field at its best. Self-sustainability was happening one step at a time.

Another critical component to sustaining life within our walls is the over seventy trees strategically planted around the property. Except for four trees planted around the playground to provide shade, they are all fruit or nut-bearing trees. They provide food for our community. The goal was to have a total of seventy in remembrance of our last property named Seventy Palms. We never want to forget our story of God's grace and provision.

Thankfully, in the last year, we have almost been able to reach our goal. The soccer field is growing grass and we finished staff housing, the basketball court, and even built a welding area and an outside team pavilion. The second dorm has its walls up with the doors and windows already set. All we needed to do was buy the chickens, finish the boy's dorm, and install a filtration system for the water. We were so close. Then COVID-19 stopped the world.

CHAPTER TWELVE

*"Life is wasted if we do not grasp the glory of
the cross, cherish it for the treasure that it is,
and cleave to it as the highest price of every
pleasure and the deepest comfort in every pain.
What was once foolishness to us—a crucified
God—must become our wisdom and our
power and our only boast in this world."*

—JOHN PIPER

THE BOOK OF ACTS DETAILS THE GROWTH and history of the
early church from Jesus' Ascension through the ministry of St.
Paul. It is twenty-eight chapters long and concludes with Paul's
arriving in Rome as a prisoner. He always desired to travel to
Rome to preach, but his arrival in chains may not have been
what he planned. Acts is the story of the early church, and
although the book in the canon of the Bible ends there, the
church's story continues. The story of God's people continues

through persecution, through attempts to eradicate it, and it has grown miraculously across the globe just as Jesus taught that it would. Jesus once told a parable about a mustard plant; though it is the smallest of seeds when planted, it becomes a large plant. He taught that this would be similar to the growth of the Kingdom of God in this world. It had humble beginnings in the Middle East but has exploded around the globe and lives on through the lives touched by the grace and mercy of Jesus. This makes me think of the story of Mission Experience. We had very humble beginnings with the goal of helping thirteen orphan children, plus adding a few in future years, but God's plans are often different than our own. The truth is that God is still writing His story.

Over the last few years, the vision for Mission Experience has grown from a thriving orphanage with a ministry of outreach to its neighbors, to much more than we had dreamed. Presently, we are working on plans to expand our ministry by building a community school and church on the additional property God has provided us. As we have lived in our neighborhood, we have observed that many children do not attend school because they cannot afford books and clothes or tuition. Mission Experience already runs a school in-house for our younger children needing education through the first few years of school. Our older children, at the Fourth-Grade educational level and above, go out to a neighboring school a few miles away. We have always thought that we would build a small school to care for our children's educational needs, but now God has laid upon us the burden to care for our neighbors. In 2020 we received our national license for our school, and it began to grow instantly. Fifteen children who were not getting educated from the neighboring Bonswa community were enrolled in our in-house school. Several of our missionaries over the years have been educators who have a heart for the children of the world, and four of them have stepped up and now are serving as the foundation for the Board of Education. Additional Haitians will be added to the board in the months to come for their local insight and direction.

A few years ago, God led a young architectural student named Natalie to attend a trip to Haiti. Since that time, she has returned several times and is now working on the school's architectural drawings. We are excited to begin this project after the work on the second dorm is complete. The school will have the capacity to hold over four hundred students. It will also provide space to educate non-traditional students like Kerby who are older but still desire to finish school. Besides classrooms, it will also have a kitchen pavilion that will allow us to provide a hot meal each day for the children and provide area for community events such as Vacation Bible School in the future. This project will enable Haitian children to grow and have opportunities while living with their parents. Several ministries are running successful schools in various parts of this county, and we hope to contribute toward the goal of advancing the educational opportunities for the children of

Haiti. This is a large task, but we are anticipating its start. This portion of our property will again be off the grid, equipped with well water and solar power. But God is not leading us to stop there.

Mission Experience has realized over the years that our ministry model based upon raising and educating the children in a safe, faith-filled environment until they reach eighteen years old would not achieve the desired outcome. We needed an exit strategy for our students, but not one that just released them back into their culture ill-prepared for success. We had to provide education and life skills but also opportunity. We needed to provide our children with the chance to learn job and business skills and the opportunity to earn a living wage. This led me to a dear old friend. Melanie is a Dean at Colorado Christian University and a local entrepreneur. I called and asked her to have lunch with me. (As you can tell, having lunch with me may alter your life.) I wanted to hear about her university program and see if there was an opportunity to take this training into the Haitian culture. She was immediately excited about the possibilities and the property that we purchased for the business center.

Today, Melanie has written an entrepreneurial training manual for the Haitian culture which teaches basic business start-up principals and translated it into Haitian Creole. She has begun a training program for our older teens and our Haitian staff which will later expand to our community. These developments have even led us to create a micro-loan program to fund these potential businesses. As of 2020, we have been able to provide three micro-loans and track those recipients' success. COVID-19 has created some difficulties along the way, but we stay committed to these programs.

The neighborhood where we live is a microcosm of the entire country. Many desire to work and take care of their family but cannot because of the lack of opportunities. Melanie teaches that thirteen percent of the people in the U.S. have what it takes to be entrepreneurs, but it is higher in developing countries out of necessity. Our hope is to provide these opportunities. We desire to educate them and give them the chance to advance with microloans and the property they need to build a business. This will provide jobs not only for the community but breathe life into inspiring entrepreneurs. We hope to throw gas on that fire. My dream is as well to build businesses that can help fund the orphanage and school providing a model that is not so dependent upon fundraising. I am praying for more entrepreneurs who do not want to just change their lives but change the world. (If you have a dream, let's go to lunch).

As we continued to evaluate our community's needs, besides the lack of education and employment opportunities, it became clear that there is another issue. The nearest medical clinic was too far away. When we were serving the neighborhood with our Vacation Bible School a few years ago one father brought his daughter seeking medical attention. The girl walked behind her father, hiding her face. When

Exhausted

ME Board of Directors;
Back row (L-R): John Krueger, John Kuhns, Steve Purkapile,
Steve Fedewa, Mike Nash, Mike Paulison
Front Row (L-R): Jessica Ramdohr, Steve Meitler,
Rebeca Duryea, Kathy Ortiz, Leslie Kotwica

Mission Team with our kids 2020

her father pulled her hand back, she looked scared, sad, and ashamed all at the same time. And she looked like she was in pain and suffering. There just happened to be an emergency room doctor from Wisconsin who was on this trip. Dr. Beth evaluated the child and realized she had a facial staph infection and simply needed a common antibiotic. Since our doctors in America had supplied us with any medications we might need while in Haiti, we had some on hand. Dr. Beth provided the girl's father with the medicine for his daughter and directions for its usage. At the end of the week, the father returned with his daughter. Her skin was already clearing up. She had a huge heart-warming smile as she thanked us. I knew in this moment that God was revealing to us another need of our community.

Now, Dr. Beth is working with us to lay the foundation to build a future medical clinic in our community. This is only in its infancy stage, as there is a lot of research on how to accomplish this goal and meet all the government requirements. It is essential for us to maintain the strong relationship we have been building with the Haitian government. We have planned two medical mission trips over the last three years but have had to cancel due to unsafe travel conditions and COVID-19. We want to build the clinic near our location and in the future employ Haitian nurses and doctors, supplementing this with medical professionals and dentists traveling from the U.S.

The Lord has continued to lead, and our community has noticed our ministry's growth. We have built a trusting relationship with the man who sold us our current property. He has been a practicing voodooist his whole life. A few years ago his wife became a Christian, but he has not been able to leave his voodoo roots. Recently, however, when the opportunity presented itself to sell some of his land, we were surprised when he did not jump at the chance. It is rare that someone would turn down the possibility to sell land with an offer of cash in front of them. His reasoning was humbling and profound. He told his would-be buyer, "I do not believe that Pastor Mike is done with all he is going to build. He is going to need more property." He decided to save the property even though we have not had a single conversation about future land.

The future success of this ministry is in God's hands. I often tell people that because of our long-term ministry strategy, we may not know if we are successful until the next generation. This may mean that our success will not be determined until long after I am gone and in heaven, which is alright because it has never depended upon me. God has propelled us beyond what we ever thought we would do and touched hearts in profound ways. I dare say it is not just the hearts and lives of Haitians that have changed. Any person invested in mission work will tell you that they have learned that mission work is never just about the locals you come to serve.

Mission work is always a two-way street. We have learned so much from the Haitian people. God is always at work in and around us. Henry Blackaby's study "Experiencing God" brought this truth home to me. Yes, God is always moving around us, but in us as well. The goal of mission trips is to help the participants get past just seeing problems to solve to also recognizing how God is moving in their own lives.

When COVID-19 hit and stopped our mission trips, we were concerned about our Haitian staff and families. We had partnered together for five years now, but now more responsibilities would rest upon them. James, his wife, and our staff stepped up in brilliant ways. They added classes for our children and kept the school going on-site through the summer for our kids so that our kids would not fall behind. They also started a nightly prayer time to pray for their country and pray for the American staff and missionaries' safety. They contacted me often to make sure everyone was safe. They organized rice and beans to give away to our neighbors. When they could no longer get out to attend church, they started a service inside the orphanage. The nannies who care for the children's needs stepped up with Kerby and led the worship music. At night during the prayer times, the nannies taught devotional messages. The music was a blessing for our families but was noticed and appreciated by our neighbors as well. James had purchased a larger speaker and each night, as they sang before their prayer time, the neighbors would listen. They thanked James and even asked him to turn it louder. These songs gave hope to our community during this world crisis and set the gospel loose in the air of our voodoo community.

COVID-19 has changed us and changed how we will

minister into the future, but we have determined to step by faith with God into whatever He has in store. There is no part of this ministry that has ever been easy. Ministry is many times more about our faithfulness to our calling than it is about our prosperity. In September of 2020, the staff, along with some board members and faithful missionaries, returned to Haiti. They were able to install a reverse osmosis system so our Haitian family could now drink the water from our well and no longer risk going out so often. Minor repairs were completed, and we stepped even closer to our goal of self-sustainability. When we started moving toward this goal over a year ago, we did not know a global pandemic was on the horizon, but God did. We do not know what challenges lay ahead, but we rest in the hands of our God who has known all along where we were headed. This is His story, and it is the story in which we continue to find ourselves in...

ACKNOWLEDGMENTS

THIS JOURNEY FROM THE BEGINNING WAS never just about me. Mission Experience is a success because of the Mission Experience family which consists of the staff, the Board, our Haitian staff, and all our missionaries who have joined us on a trip. We have an amazingly high rate of short-term return missionaries. Several of them are considered unpaid staff because they have become leaders in specific segments of our ministry. Some of the names in this book have been changed for sake of identity.

I have so many people who not only helped me with the writing of this book but who have lived this with me. My story is their story. And our stories are God's. At times they leaned on me and my faith, and other times I have rested on them and their faith. I cannot tell you how much I love and appreciate them.

My first thank you is to my family. Ellie has been an amazing partner in ministry and life. I could never do this without her. Her love for the Haitian children is incredible, and her faith stands as a beacon to my own. She is their "mom." My three girls, Abigail, Maddie, and McKenzie have walked this whole journey with me. They have been through the ups and downs and at times sat at home praying about their father's safety. I am sorry for the times you have had to worry. I could not have raised three young ladies with whom I am prouder and love. Their hearts to impact the world is awe-inspiring. Also, I want to thank my mother, Nadine Paulison, for her gift of faith and my father, Edward J. Paulison, for his heart to serve those in need. My life is a combination of theirs.

The staff of Mission Experience has been an integral part of who we are. You have met many of the staff in the pages of this book, but there are others paid and unpaid. I want to thank our present staff for taking the journey with me and for the integrity of their faith. We could have never done it without any of them. Thank you to Doug and Leslie Kotwica, Ellie Paulison, Stuart and Regina Pederson, Kailee Duryea, and Kim Garcia. Kailee is the newest member of our staff but has been part of the Mission Experience family for years and lived through many of these events. I also want to thank our Haitian staff: James and Edeline, Casimir, Jacklin, Bernadette, Celie, Madeline, Silone, Wideline, Deulifait, Kerby, Jordany, and our social worker, Alain. They are family and have done a fantastic job for us. I love them all.

I also want to thank all those who have served on our Board of Directors past and present. Mission Experience is a family, and this board is much more than a figurehead. They have traveled to and from Haiti, sweated on work teams, and put in countless hours praying and attempting to discern God's will together. I appreciate all of those who started this journey and had the faith to walk through the initial storms: Ron Wentzel, Warren Abraham, Kimberly Baldwin, Karen Smith, Dr. Bryan and Melanie Scheer, and Percy Harris. Thank you to those who continue to serve today and those who have joined the present Board of Directors: Mike Nash, Rebecca Duryea, John Kuhns, John Krueger, Steve Purkipile, Steve Fedewa, Steve Meitler, Kathy Ortiz, and Jessica Ramadohr. Thank you to those who are serving the Board of Education Board of Directors as we prepare to build the school: Albert Ambling, Teri Lynn Schragg, Jana Horn, and Kristen Bauer. Lastly, thank you to Dr. Beth Griffen who is partnering with us on the dream of the medical clinic. She and her husband, Dan, have been incredible supporters of our ministry.

A special thank you to those who worked with me on this book. Thank you to Skip Vogel, a mentor of mine, and to John Kuhns and Ellie for being content readers and making sure I had facts and dates right. Thank you to Emily Fedewa, Adam Abraham, and Karen Smith who served as editors. And a special thank you to Ty Saucerman, and Percy and Barbara Harris. Ty is my accountability partner with whom I have met weekly for years. Percy has been my personal prayer partner through all of this. He and Barbara have walked with me and supported me personally for years. I could never have done this without any of them.

There are so many others that I could thank, but I am sure that I will miss someone on the list. You all know how valuable you are to Mission Experience and how much I love and appreciate you. Your faith and your hearts of service and dedication have allowed us to take our vision way beyond what we could have ever imagined. Thank You! And all praise to our Creator God. You have preserved and sustained us. Each step of the way, You have proven Yourself faithful. Thank You, Father!

ABOUT THE AUTHOR

REV. DR. MICHAEL PAULISON (PASTOR MIKE) has been in ministry for over 30 years. He has served congregations in Colorado and always worked with the poor from New York City to Colorado, including mission trips around the US and the globe. He is the founder and Director of Mission Experience. When not in Haiti, he travels around the country sharing his story. If you would like him to come share an update, please see the contact information at the back of the book.

FOR FURTHER STUDY

Could God be calling you to participate in missions?

FIRST, IF YOU ARE A CHILD OF GOD, our missionary God is calling you. I do not know if it is for overseas work, but it is to participate in His mission. Over my thirty years in ministry the most often asked question is "What is God's will for my life?" I may not know a specific answer for you, but I can tell you God's call upon your life is to join Him in His mission wherever you are. If you begin there, the rest of God's purposes will unfold.

Begin by reading Isaiah 58. Notice how God defines a true fast. What components of these verses speak to you?

Scripture mentions caring for the poor, widows, and orphans over twenty times. Read Deuteronomy 15:10–11, Proverbs 3:27–28, 28:27, 31:8–9, Isaiah 1:17, James 1:27, and 1 John 3:17. What written in these verses speaks to you?

Read Matthew 25:31–46. This is the last judgement

separation of the sheep and the goats. As you read, do not highlight just the judgement section. Notice that the sheep were unaware of their deeds. They simply were living out their faith and God noticed.

God is calling you to join Him in His mission of living and sharing His love for this world expressed in the life, death and resurrection of His Son, Jesus. Do not do this out of guilt! Learn to live out of the overflow of God's love for you. As you have read in the pages of this book, this may not be an easy journey, but it is impossible in your own strength and if you are led by guilt. St. Paul writes that the Spirit of God compelled him to preach the Gospel (1 Cor. 9:16). Is God stirring your heart right now, and do you feel His prompting to be God's vessel of love in this world? Then maybe it is time...Be careful. It may change your life forever.

—**Pastor Mike**

ENDNOTES

1. Pallardy, Richard. 2010 Haiti Earthquake, https://www.britannica.com/event/2010-Haiti-earthquake.

2. Petro Caribe Scandal-Petro Caribe was a strategic oil alliance between Venezuela and Haiti. This agreement allows Haiti to receive oil from Venezuela and defer payment for up to twenty-five years. Two billion dollars disappeared from this fund, and the President has been accused of misappropriating it.

ADDITIONAL RESOURCES

FOR MORE PURCHASING OPTIONS AND INFORMATION on the book, visit the publisher at www.tenthpowerpublishing.com.

If you want to learn more about Mission Experience, receive their monthly newsletter, join them on a trip, or become a monthly donor, please visit www.missionexperience.org. Or feel free to email the author at mike.e.paulison@gmail.com. You can also follow on Facebook, Twitter, or Snapchat.